"THEY TOLD ME"

"They told me I wouldn't live to be 2 yrs. old because they found me starving on someone's porch....

I'm 55 now....

They told me I wasn't smart enough and that I didn't need a higher education......

I have an AA, BS and MS.

They told me I would never be part of anything worthwhile.

I'm a member of MD-Military-Holding-Lodge-No--122 - MWPHGL of Maryland, The Monday Cub (Oldest Social Club for African American Men in Delaware and maybe the Nation-1876) recently resigned, The Drill Sergeant Association, and Bethel AME Church to name a few.

They told me the Army wasn't the way to go and I was wasting my time and the organization wouldn't teach me anything.

I was Squad Leader, Platoon Sergeant, Detachment NCOIC,

CID Investigator, Drill Sergeant and an EO Advisor for 5,000 Soldiers and Civilians just to name a few, it has taught me a lot.

They told me I couldn't run a full marathon.

I finished in the top half.

They told me I was too small for martial arts.

I received a 2nd degree black belt in Hapkido and a Red Sash (Chamber 5) in Kung-Fu.

They told me that I will fail in life.

The lord has blessed me with a lovely wife, 4 grown men (sons), a lovely Stepdaughter, and 6 grandchildren. It was rough getting there but I'm here." (Started from the bottom).

They told me I would never, never find my bloodline.

Well, I found my birth mother, father, sisters and brothers and a host of cousins and combined my bloodline to my family that raised me and taught me everything I needed to know about life altogether into one big happy family.

I now have two mothers and fathers.

THANK YOU FOR TELLING ME THOSE THINGS.....................

KEEP YOUR HEAD UP, AND LIVE YOUR DREAMS, MAKE NO EXCUSES............

Kevin I.J.A. Barnett, Sr

Dedicated to
William J. Barnett & Muriel C. Barnett
Lois Hodge Bean & George Niblack

For my sons,
Kevin J. Barnett, Jr.
Isaiah J. Barnett
Charles B.C.D. Boling
Darrius J. Barnett

For my stepdaughter
Samantha L. Justice

For my grandchildren,
Saniah
Iquan
Kevin
Isaiah
Zuri
Ki'Re

Rest in Peace,
Delores Stewart
Andre Daniels
Brandon Barnett
Velta Smith Pelham
Joseph Carter

Photographs by
Samantha L. Justice
Charlene Terry

Table of Contents

PART THREE: EXITING MY SHADOWS

FAMILY PHOTOS

PART ONE:

WHO AM I?

This beginning part is rough to tell.
But this is my story.

MY SHADOWS

Can you imagine a mother
giving up a child
and then never seeing that child
again?

Would that mother
visit the child
in her dreams?
Would she spin out
anguished fantasies
about the life
she and the child might have had?

And what about
that lost child?
Is it possible for that child
to not believe
they did something bad,
something wrong,
to deserve this?

How could a mother
do that to a child
she carried for nine months,
and not contact that child
ever again,
forever...

CHAPTER I:

UNWANTED

Being abandoned as a baby hurt.

It hurt like hell. No doubt about it.

No mother. No father. No sisters. No brothers.

No future. No past. No roots. No home.

Nobody wanted me. And why? Man, I didn't have a clue.

So what do you do? Where do you go, when from the minute you're born you've been cast into the shadows? When the records of your birth family are locked up and kept secret? When every single day you grapple with the sucker punch of living your whole life not knowing who your mother and father are? Whether you have any siblings? Any aunts or uncles? A grandmother or grandfather? And where they are?

When you don't even know who *you* are?

———◆———

Being unwanted is like living in the shadows.

For the first 50 years of my life, my shadows were about all I had.

Abandoned by my birth mother…unwanted by my birth father…left to die out on the street…shuttled from foster home to foster home…growing up defenseless against the abuse and neglect of my foster parents…

Man, I was a shadow nobody wanted from the start.

But I made a vow that no matter what happened in my life, I'd claw my way out of those shadows.

Sure, there were times when the punishment my body and mind had been put through took me right to the edge of breaking that vow. But instead of giving up, I pushed through the pain, and pursued my dreams. Along the way, I got some good breaks and some bad ones. I got my share of scars and some of the cruel circumstances I faced broke my heart. What can I tell you?

It's like the great black writer Maya Angelou once said:

"There is no greater agony than bearing an untold story inside of you."

And the poet Langston Hughes could have been writing about me, when he said: "Life for me ain't been no crystal stair…"

CHAPTER 2:

BAD MILK

This is the way the story of my birth was told to me.

According to the story, I was brought into this world on July 30, 1960 by a woman named Ms. Hodge. That's the way I heard it from my second foster parent, Mrs. K. Crawford. Mrs. Crawford stuck with that story until the day she passed away.

As the story goes, the minute I came out of the womb my mother gave me over to the medical personnel—she never even looked at me. She stated in the record books that she couldn't take care of me because of the other children she bore. Maybe so. I guess this was a bad thing during the 1950s as far as having children without being married goes.

My first foster parents didn't even last a year. I'm not kidding. They wrapped in a blanket and took me to another part of town. Then they left me on somebody's front porch, with a bottle of bad milk. I never saw them again. I was out there in the bitter cold and the wind for about two days with that bottle of milk. I was dehydrated. Cold. Shivering. My little arms were shrunken to nothing but bone.

I was knocking at death's door until a social worker found me. She rushed my little tiny self to the hospital. The doctors there had to feed me through my ankles because I couldn't open my mouth to drink. Today I still have those scars.

I never did find out why my first foster parents were so cold-hearted. I guess they just no longer wanted to take care of me. So I was basically left to die on somebody's porch with that bottle of spoiled milk, until a social worker found me.

When I think back to that time, I am beset with pain, rage and heartache. What compelled my birth mother to abandon me? Where did she go? Why did she leave me? Did she think she was leaving me into a better life? And what about my first foster mother? Did she really leave me to die alone? Or did she think I'd be taken, cuddled, and protected into some other woman's bosom?

Reminds me of the story of Moses.

Now I don't compare myself to Moses in the Bible, but my dark little tale has some similarities to his. Moses was supposed to be drowned in the River Nile, but was adopted by the Pharaoh's daughter. Once Moses learned the truth, he wondered about his birth mother, and her anguish. And Moses had a quest. Of course, I don't plan to lead anyone to the Promised Land. But something about Moses wandering through the wilderness on what should have been an 11-day journey that took Moses 40 years sure hits home with me.

Just like Moses, being given up at birth wasn't the first nor the end of my troubles. My shadows continued to haunt me with nightmares of torture and abuse at a young age. It was only later that I realized, just like Moses, that the truth about my whole life had been hidden behind secrets.

CHAPTER 3:

MY EARLY SHADOWS

After being left to die, and then put into several foster homes, I was finally placed in the home of Mr. & Mrs. Crawford, at 218 Amherst Street in East Orange, New Jersey.

The Crawfords were an elderly black couple who needed to supplement their fixed income. Now I don't know how qualified they were to be foster parents. Maybe somebody in social services shoulda checked into that, before placing me there. But the system's so overburdened that I bet folks like the Crawfords just slipped through the cracks.

They weren't bad people—they just didn't care about me one damn bit.

DFAS also placed another young man into their home. His name was Maurice.

Maurice was a light-skinned young boy. This was always thrown in my face by Mrs. Crawford. Because of my dark skin she'd tell me I was sinful and ugly. I was the devil's child, that is why my birth mother gave me up. "You are ignorant, lazy and dumb," she'd tell me.

She made me feel worthless all right. Like a big fat zero.

I resented the double-standard, but I never blamed Maurice. I figured if I just kept myself out of trouble, things were bound to get better. Man, was I wrong!

I was treated like a slave. The Crawfords always kept their house clean—not a speck of dust anywhere. So it was up to me to keep the floors clean, which I had to do every day on my hands and knees.

My bedroom was actually in the dining area, where I slept on a cot. Maurice slept in the same bedroom as Mrs. Crawford. I got the point real fast: things were going to be tough for a darker-skinned black kid like me.

I was never allowed to watch TV under the watchful eye of Mrs. Crawford. Technically, the only time I could watch TV was when she was asleep. I had to sneak over to the set by crawling on my hands and knees while Maurice would hold the family dog away from biting and attacking me. Then I'm trying to watch the glowing tube of the TV and all the while this dog is snarling at top volume. Snorting and snarling not five feet away from me. Then when my show was finished, back to the cot I'd crawl, only to lie awake most of the night listening to Maurice and Mrs. Crawford snoring down the hallway.

The Crawfords' dog's name was Silver. Just thinking about that dog now gives me an intense feeling of anger. Silver was a white dog— a mutt, with brownish spots—and one mean-ass dog. In one powerful leap he could rip your throat out. They kept him tied up at the back door to the basement. No one ever paid attention to him. He barked and snarled all the time. Only person he greeted joyously was his master, Mr. Crawford.

Silver seemed to like Maurice too, but he couldn't stand me. The Crawfords trained him to be that way. Maurice would take him for walks and was allowed to play with him while I was tied up with an extension cord strapped to Mr. Crawford's hand, like his pet slave. Even today, I can feel the skintight grip of that cord wrapped around my throat. Choking me.

I remember Maurice would come and untie me when the old man was sleeping. We used to sneak out and play stickball in the street with a broomstick and a ball made of aluminum foil. The sewer cover would be home base.

Maurice helped me get through a lot of the crap that I had to go through. Maurice had his own problems, mind you, probably stemming from being an unwanted foster kid, like me. But Maurice was cool.

I never did understand how these poor black folks ended up with us kids. I guess it was their way to make money. Living with the Crawfords was like living with two drill sergeants. No matter which of us kids did something that went against their rules, the spotlight would always be on me. I mean, why me? They made me feel like the worst child that was ever born.

And if me or Maurice *really* did something bad—God have mercy on me.

Once when I was laying on my cot, Mr. Crawford snuck up and attacked me with the belt. He whipped me and lashed me and beat me so hard I had belt marks all over my body. For days I could barely sit on the toilet.

And for what? I still don't know!

I'm sure Mr. Crawford thought he was raising us kids in his household right. But in his house, Mr. Crawford's word was the law. And he didn't care one bit if he had to resort to near-constant verbal and physical abuse, or rolling his sleeves up to beat me or Maurice, to keep the law.

Every day at the Crawfords was a nightmare. But holidays were the worst for me. I felt invisible during the holidays.

I remember my first Christmas there. Maurice and I got up early because we wanted to see what we received from "Santa Claus." I raced over to the couch and was warned not to go there because those toys, those gifts *weren't mine*. I was told to go sit in my chair because I wasn't a good boy. I was a bad person and that's why I only had a couple of gifts compared to my foster brother.

Now most people love Christmas and gift-giving. But I really hated Christmas, because it wasn't Christmas for me. Maurice always got more toys, because they told me I was a troublemaker, I was bad, and Santa Claus was going to get me. All this was because of the color of my skin. And this from my black foster parents! It was their way of keeping me under their control.

And Halloween? Halloween wasn't the best time for me either. I was the devil most of the time while Maurice was Superman, Batman, or some other superhero. To this day I really don't like to get into those two holidays because of my past and the way people treat each other during that time of the year. I mean most folks give for the wrong reason, thinking that they should get something in return.

One thing I did like about that time of the year was all the baseball and football cards I received. Those cards help me get through a lot.

My favorites were my baseball cards.

I had Willie Mays, Hank Aaron, Roberto Clemente, Harmon Killebrew—all these old-school Hall of Fame baseball players. During the time I was left alone I used to take my baseball cards and put them out on the living room rug according to their positions.

I'd put the Clemente card in right field.

Willie Mays in center.

Hank Aaron in left.

I would take a pencil and use it as a bat, then grab a piece of tin foil, ball it up, and use it as a ball. If I hit the ball in the kitchen—BOOM!—that would be a home run.

Willie Mays was the card that stood out the most. Willie stood out because—well, because he was Willie Mays, the Say Hey Kid, a very charismatic outfielder for the Giants. So I always tried to pretend that Willie Mays card was me, running back to make a catch, or hitting the ball into the kitchen for a home run. Willie's card always had the most home runs. So that card got through a lot of bad times. When nobody was home that's what I used to do. And because I didn't have a happy life or a way to escape my unhappy one, I made one up.

CHAPTER 4:

THE DREAM MAN

Mrs. Crawford never did let me sass her. Every day I'd wake to the shattering blast of her voice, blaming me for something. Even now, my stomach begins to churn, remembering all the times I got beat.

They'd get on me for not doing things right around the house. I'd open my mouth to protest and Mrs. Crawford would warn me not to talk back or I'd get a beating. I started to get the feeling this woman was stone cold crazy. She never tried to be a mother, or even a substitute for a mother, to provide love or comfort. She seemed to take pleasure in hurting me. Even as a kid, I had an inkling that the violence and abuse I experienced at the Crawfords was out of the ordinary, but my hunches weren't confirmed until years later.

Sleeping was a challenge also at the Crawfords. Fact is, it was impossible.

I'd lie on my little cot, and thrash through my thoughts,

searching for some kind of hope for my life. Things'd get so bad, I used to knock on the wall and call the Dream Man to come and put me to sleep. My knees and my feet would knock together and I would just go into a dream world. That's how I was able to deal with all the abuse and mistreatment. To this day I still do that every now and then. I couldn't wait to go to bed back then, even though I had to hit the pillow around 7:30.

In the privacy of my bed, I felt safe. My bed gave me a sanctuary, a place to go with all my longing and sadness. It helped me travel in my mind miles and miles away from the Crawfords', and in the hands of the Dream Man I felt protected. The Dream Man was my refuge, a place for me to lay my burdens down.

Still, I'd get beatings for nothing. Seemed like as soon as I opened my eyes each morning I'd be getting a beating.

Over time, I'd cocoon further and further into myself. The nightmares were so intense that I started getting headaches. I'd get these headaches—a sharp, knifelike stab that made my breathing shallow. It was a chronic condition that would continue to afflict me for years.

When my brain wanted to give up, and the fears I couldn't control overcame me, I'd put my head mentally in another place, and my dreams saved me. All I had to do was survive from dinner until the night, when I could hit the bed.

Which brings me to eating at the Crawfords.

Every meal they made me sit in this red chair. I had a bright red chair at the corner of the kitchen. It was this hard, wooden chair with three slats. An old-ass, uncomfortable-to-sit-in chair. Their goal was always to make me as uncomfortable as possible. But I loved that chair for some unknown reason. I felt safe once I was sitting there. If I wasn't spending time in my sleep area or being tied up by Mr. Crawford, I was sitting in my little red chair.

I remember the times when my foster brother would sneak seconds to me at the dinner table—I was never allowed to have seconds—but once Mr. and Mrs. Crawford were out of sight Maurice would slide me a little something extra. He was the bomb! He helped me get through a lot of the crazy stuff that was going on in that house.

School was okay. It was a place for me to learn and I felt I was safe there, until I got beat up by this young kid that we say today was "girlish." He took my raincoat and kicked it all the way home. Then when I came in the house to tell my foster parents I got beat by them for bringing home a dirty coat.

Truth is, because of what was going on at home I didn't do too well in school. I had to be kept back in the first grade, and I didn't pay attention because of things I was going through. My life for the first 8 years was always the same—worrying about getting beat, then getting beat, and worrying about more beatings. Eating at the dinner table never changed, and Christmas and Halloween always sucked. That stuff that happened back in the 60s took a lot to get over. Yep. Hard times.

Oh and one more thing: the names they called me. The name calling never stopped.

They called me "Negro." They called me "Black Nigger." They called me "Ugly," and "No-Good." For some damn reason, my nickname at the Crawfords was "Skeeter." That's the name they gave me—I have no idea why. My real name was almost never mentioned. I actually knew that Skeeter was my name before I knew my name was Kevin!

I thought I would never leave that place. But I had dreams and my dreams gave me hope, and that's what kept me going.

There was no running away from the nightmares at 218 Amherst Street. It was only after I was finally out of the Crawfords' house that I fully realized the terror I felt in my soul. The Dream Man did his best to soothe my worried mind and take away my fears. But he couldn't take them all.

CHAPTER 5:

THE FIGHTER

I did have one hero during that time. It was the boxer, the heavyweight fighter Muhammad Ali.

During the 60s it was amazing to see a young black man stand up for what he thought was right. Ali was a champion and he was controversial and he was courageous and he was larger than life. He had an impact on the world and on other black kids like me. Ali was my hero and I wanted to be him.

In the ring, nobody could touch Ali. He could "float like a butterfly and sting like a bee" and he was The Greatest. And he spent a lifetime living up to that legend. Fortunately for me, Mr. Crawford sometimes let me watch Ali on TV. As a young man, Mr. Crawford used to make me sit between his legs while we watched the television. That was his way of not letting me get away.

Mr. Crawford used to tie me up with an extension cord, around my wrist or around my neck, and sit me between his legs to watch television. The whole time we're sitting there, I'd feel my heart pounding out of my chest, and a sharp pain that restricted my breathing, worried that for some damn reason or other I'd get a whipping or a beating, for something me or Maurice had done.

I truly think Mr. Crawford relished the fear he put in me. He'd squint up his eyes and watch me out of the corner of them suspiciously. So even while he and I are cozied up to the TV I'm afraid for my life, and under constant stress. I was barely able to focus on what's on the screen.

Meanwhile Mr. Crawford would be grunting and grumbling and hissing about the evening news. He'd complain about the President, or the war in Vietnam—which it was obvious, from the way he tightened his fist around the extension cord wrapped around my neck, that I was responsible for.

Every Saturday afternoon though, no matter what else was on, he'd stop everything to watch one program: ABC's Wide World of Sports. And believe it or not, the thing we watched together most often was Muhammad Ali. And immediately I was hooked on him: Ali was a very handsome guy, nut-brown in color, muscular and trim. He was also an incredibly sharp dresser, and his grooming was immaculate. What that said to me was that even a raggedy kid like me had a chance to be something, and anything was possible. To me Ali was a superhero who could do it all.

Ali was everywhere you looked back then. I was always hearing and seeing his every move, punch, jab, and knockout. I also used to see how Ali would talk back to the media about getting out of the Vietnam War, or talking about civil rights and stuff, and how he'd express his feelings about things, and make these bold predictions about his fights. Like how if he was going to knock you out in the 8th round, BOOM! He'd knock you out in the 8th round.

Every time I heard him talking like that, it made my jaw drop. As a black individual in the 60s, someone talking back to the media, the Establishment, White Society, that was unheard of! And so just sitting there and seeing how he was so courageous and confident in talking to the masses built confidence in me.

So as I was going through this dreadful period and tied up with an extension cord next to Mr. Crawford, I had Muhammad Ali on my mind. I was going to make sure somehow I survived. I was going to make sure one day I had a good home. I was going to make sure I got a college education. "I'm going to be somebody," I'd tell myself. "I'm not going to let anybody call me ugly or stop me from being successful because I'm black." So I decided to take all the negatives happening in my situation and use that as motivation for the rest of my life.

I'm not going to use my past an excuse not to succeed.

All this from watching how Muhammad Ali handled his life.

But my life was really death. I had nothing to live for. My foster parents were cruel and crazy, and they didn't love me all. It made it hard for me to trust anybody. I lacked confidence in myself. I didn't look anyone in the eye because I thought that I would get slapped.

This type of thing was my life up until Mr. Crawford died. I was 9 or 10 years old. He died of hiccups. Weird, right? The man *died of hiccups*. He wound up going to the hospital with hiccups, and the next thing I knew somebody said he was gone. Just like that.

First time I heard the news, I thought to myself: *Nah, he ain't dead. Just trying to trick me, and cause me another beating.* Then a light flashed on in my head—*wait, maybe this dude is dead*—and as soon as I thought it, I was trying to hide the smile on my face. Soon as I realized the news about his death was for real, I started grinning even more.

Right then I knew: there's gotta be a God.

To me, hearing Mr. Crawford had died of the hiccups was a sweet sound. It made me wanna dance. He was the only person whose death I actually celebrated. I hated him. I hated him more than Mrs. Crawford because basically Mrs. Crawford was carrying out the terrible things Mr. Crawford told her to do.

The man never had a kind word for me at all—not "I love you" or "you're good" or anything. He wouldn't even speak to me. So the day he died I was so damn happy; he didn't deserve to live on this planet.

Which explains the other thing I remember about his death.

The day he went to the hospital, I remember black-eyed peas was involved, in some kinda way. Like it was his last meal. So nowadays I try not to eat black-eyed peas. It's not that I don't like black-eyed peas, mind you, 'cuz black-eyed peas are pretty good—but when I see 'em that's the only time I think about him.

After he was gone, and old Mr. Crawford had breathed his last breath, Mrs. Crawford tried to keep the same control on us. But it didn't work. I started running my mouth at her. I would sass her, and talk back, then run and hide under the dining room table. She'd point her skinny finger at me and scream. She would always threaten me with calling DFAS, which I wanted her to do. *Go ahead,* I thought to myself while she was chasing me, *please pick up the phone and call!*

I was trying to get her to call Social Services, so they would take me out of the house.

One day she did call. And the social worker came, and I told her some things that were going on. But nothing happened, and I still lived in fear of getting slapped or smacked or cracked in the head.

That was more or less my life. It never flashed on me that things would get any better. Until one day, when I heard I was being sent to meet my new family. And let me tell you, when the day came for me to say my final goodbye to the house at 218 Amherst Street, I didn't shed one tear. Hell no. I was ready.

CHAPTER 6:

HEAVEN

My new family was the Barnetts. Living with them was my Heaven, my Kingdom Come, my Promised Land. It was like the Land of Milk and Honey and Disneyland, all rolled into one.

I had no idea what I was in store for, when I met the Barnetts. Their names were Bill and Muriel. I was sent way across town, about 20 or 30 minutes from where I grew up with the Crawfords.

As I was driving there, with the social worker, I started to see that things didn't seem the same. The cars were different. They were bigger and nicer. The buildings were newer and shinier. It didn't look old and run-down, like my old neighborhood.

Once I got there, and was carrying my suitcase up the front steps, the place just looked and smelled like home. It was like the new place put its arms around me and walked me right through the front door. I remember standing on the front steps, and noticing what real green grass was like. I'm talking *manicured* grass. The Barnetts had a big landscaped front yard, and it was clean, and a park right across the street. So the fact that the social worker was taking me to this new foster home, after all them years in what felt like was prison lockup, was like *wow*, this is unreal, this is *heaven*.

This was the beginning of life to me.

On the first morning I woke in my new home, all I wanted to do was wander the streets, gazing at all the buildings and the green lawns. Mr. Barnett, my new father, was tall, and everybody said he looked like a young Bill Cosby. He was the kind of man who said a lot without words. He'd come up to me, at the dinner table or while I'm watching TV, and pat me on the back, or affectionately rub the top of my head, just to show how he noticed me. I'd look for a frown, or a cussing out or a slap on the skull. But there never was one.

And my mother—my new mother was beautiful. I thought they was like rich, because I came from a home where the individuals were 65, 68 years old. These people were vibrant, and young, and making eye contact with me, and telling me "We want you to be part of this family." And here I was, just meeting them!

This family was everything I dreamed of and more. I was sorry to leave my foster brother Maurice but man, I was happy to leave 218 Amherst Street behind.

Living with my new family was great. Mrs. Barnett was fair—she treated everyone as special, me included. It's like she knew I was a good kid, and not this wild-ass bad kid the Crawfords' stories probably painted me as.

At first I was hit hard with this wave of uncertainty. Like, can I really be this lucky? Or is all this love everybody's pouring on me just another trick? Then I was like a kid in a candy store! And now my dreams of living a better life began to kick into overdrive.

They gave me my own room, and the freedom to walk around without fear. I was able to go the park and the playground all by myself. Nobody watching over me and my every step was like *amazing!* Just going out the front door, just stepping outside the house by myself, was *amazing*. Everything seemed like an answer to my prayers. It seemed like a dream. But it was *real*. So I told myself I didn't want to do anything that would mess my chances or my situation up. 'Cuz I didn't want to go back to the Crawfords, no way!

I had two siblings that were also living there with me. My little foster sister and brother. In my mind, they were already my family. I felt loved, but didn't really know how to express it. I was so battered and beat up and quiet at the Crawfords. I didn't know how to respond to folks who actually cared. I was shy, and I always looked mean, I guess. And I guess I didn't talk a lot in the beginning.

Our conversations in the beginning were mostly one-sided. They talked. I listened. Probably didn't say much than a sentence or two, those first couple of weeks.

But that didn't seem to matter. Somehow my new parents understood that my shyness was not an ordinary shyness— that it was based on this brutal terror I felt in my bones, from always feeling scared and guilty around the Crawfords. So they gently began to push me out of my old comfort zone.

My new Dad took an immediate interest in me. He taught

me how to play sports. That is correct—I was finally able to call someone *Dad!* This was very hard for me, because of all the stories that the Crawfords told me about my biological family. Mrs. Crawford used to tell me that my mother hated me, that she hated the fact that I was born, she didn't want me.

"That's why you're with us," Mrs. Crawford told me, "and she'll never come back for you. There will always be someone who doesn't want you. The only reason we got you is because we get money for you." Things like that. She said you'll never see your real mother and father again. She would just pound that into me. Shouting and cursing at me for being such a stupid kid that nobody wanted.

No one had ever put a hand on my shoulder to steer me in the right direction.

So it was kinda hard to call Mr. Barnett my "Dad."

For the first years of my life, I'd survived without a Dad. My fundamental responsibility in life had been to protect myself; now here I had somebody promising to protect me!

I can't explain the waves of relief that flooded me. For awhile, I felt these moments of terror that this safe and normal childhood the Barnetts were offering me would suddenly disappear, and I'd be back to living a nightmare. I'd think to myself: *This is too good to be true*, and I'd shut my hopes down. That was my only defense. I had no emotions, so it was hard to show emotions to anybody. I was the kind of person who would never smile, and be standoffish. And my father trying to love on me was hard, because I had built up these walls. And they had no idea the kind of things I had gone through, in the first 10 years of my life. It was a climb and a struggle for me to let anybody inside that wall.

And now here this man was teaching me things that I thought I would never learn.

I was passionate about sports, everything from ping pong to baseball and basketball. Whatever sport was in season, I wanted to play it. What my new Dad did was he spent a lot of time with me, teaching me to hit a baseball, to throw—I owe that to him. He put a basketball into my hands and it was like magic the first time I touched a basketball. He showed me how to shoot, dribble and run. I even shot like he did and the ball went in. Soon as I made that first shot, I glanced quickly at my Pop, and he was beaming. He was smiling like any normal, happy dad should be.

And when I did something wrong my new Pops was cool, and as long as I 'fessed up he'd let me off without punishment. "All right, son," he'd say in this calm voice, "just don't let there be a next time."

No beating. No whupping. No hollering. Nothing terrible happened. Life went on.

It was almost miraculous.

The truth is I knew this was my chance, maybe my last chance, to make something better of my life.

My new home also got me more connected with the meaning of family.

My Pop's sister had three children of her own, and we became real close. I spent the night over there a lot. We rode bikes together back and forth from Newark to East Orange, which you really can't do these days. I went to the zoo and ranches to see animals. I also was watching TV all by myself now. I'd watch *Sanford and Son. Batman. Superman.* Even stuff like *Dynasty.* Having all that control to watch whatever I wanted was unbelievable. Having dinner, and breakfast, was even better. I was served the same time as everyone else. I also was able to get seconds. This took a while for me to get used to.

Once I was enrolled in school I was feeling like I died and went to heaven. The only thing I didn't like about the new school was the teasing of me being different than my new family. Children can be rough even if they didn't know the real deal of a situation. I was teased about my last name and why I didn't have the same last name as my family. I also was skinny because of my past. But I was really good in basketball, and I started to make friends which I never had back in the old days.

Every now and then I did spend time wondering about my birth mother. About what happened to her. I'd see her in my dreams. I'd wonder if she had any other kids, and what their names were. I'd dream about the life we might have had. I'd wonder when she was coming to get me. But mostly those feelings were overshadowed in the old days by all the anger and unhappiness and meanness I felt living with the Crawfords, so I tuned that stuff out and concentrated on the happy life I'd been blessed with the Barnetts, which made me happier than anything I could have dreamt. The fact that I had a family like I never had back at the Crawfords made me feel like a king.

CHAPTER 7:

TIME FOR LIVIN'

The family started to take in other young men that were in my situation, but out of all of them I knew I was special. The Barnetts always treated me like I was special, so basically it didn't matter if they brought in other children, I figured I'd be staying with them for the long haul.

I knew I was blessed and privileged to be raised by the Barnetts—but not all of my siblings felt the same way.

My oldest brother got in trouble with the law. He even robbed us during church service. Check this: My grandmother started the church in her house. It grew, and my brother had brought some people over to the house one day, and while folks were having church these guys ransacked the place. My brother and sister had these big tall coin banks, shaped like poodles. They might have had 2 or 300 dollars in there, in coins. My brother and his friends took all that, robbed the house, and left. He was a problem with the law all the time.

He didn't appreciate what the Barnetts were doing for him.

But man, I did.

I was trusted with everything at the Barnetts. My adopted brothers and sister, they always looked up to me as the oldest one. When Mrs. Barnett had my younger brother Wade, and they brought him home, I was able to change his diapers and all that baby stuff, so it was like my life had come full circle. I had responsibility at the Barnetts, I was trusted with something, whereas I was never trusted with *anything* at the Crawfords. Being trusted, that never woulda happened.

My Mom actually did homework with me. She did it through the 8th grade. As I grew older, I excelled in sports. When I was at the Crawfords I used to dream about becoming a pro athlete. But I never played basketball or football because of my fear of them. That all changed when my new father put a basketball into my hands. So many doors opened up. Graduating from the 8th grade was such a big thing. My new Mom and Dad came to see me and I made them proud and I was proud.

My teenage years just flew by. It was my time for livin'. We were brought up in church. This was one of the reasons I couldn't play ball anymore on Sundays. My grandma was a pastor; my Dad was assistant pastor and my Mom was an evangelist.

Church was stuffed down our throats. Today, I think that may have been a good thing, but growing up it was hard.

Here's the schedule: 9 a.m. Sunday school; 11:00 worship; and that usually ended around 4 p.m. The 7:30 Sunday night service lasted until 10 p.m. Monday we had to go to the senior citizen home to visit and have prayer from 7:30 to 9 a.m. Tuesdays were for evening prayer. Wednesday was Bible class from 7 to 9:30 p.m. Thursday was "YPE" which means "Young People's Endeavor" from 7:30 to 9:30. Friday night service was held from 7:30 to 10 p.m. and Saturdays we went to downtown Newark for street service.

This was my schedule from 9th to 12th grade. There was a lot of pressure on me to become a minister. I had to learn the Bible from back to back, side to side and all points in between. I preached up and down 95, throughout Newark. All the while I wondered what life was like outside of church. I wanted to go to college but my grandmother didn't think that was necessary. I wanted to go into the Army after I graduated from high school but my father made it known that that was not going to happen.

That was pretty much how things went, until 1973.

Between church and going to school, I became involved in martial arts. My grandmother thought martial arts was of the devil, so I had some challenges when it came to learning. I started to take an interest in martial arts and Bruce Lee—the kung-fu king who had just die—became my hero after Muhammad Ali. The thing I admired about Bruce Lee was he was *small*. He was only about 140 pounds but he was very powerful—not just in his arms and legs but powerful in his thinking, in his philosophies, and I would read all the different things he would write, like different proverbs, books, and taoisms. Because of him, and because I was small like him, when I had to fight I fought bigger fighters just like him. So when I found myself losing or I couldn't get through some bigger dude's defense I found myself going back to "What would Bruce Lee do?"

So that's why those two guys—Bruce Lee and Muhammad Ali—were my heroes. Because of their lack of size. Because of who they were. Because of people telling them they can't do something, and that pushed them, so that pushed me to get through that part of my life until I could have a real father, who became my real hero.

That outlook helped when one of the other major things happened to me while I was in high school.

I had a seizure.

This was caused by some of the stuff that happened to me when I was younger. I'd get this seizure, where I would black out a little bit. I used to have nightmares, about the bad things that took place in my life. I'd have these thoughts about the Crawfords coming back to get me. I'd get headaches and worry about them putting me back in the foster care system. It put some negative feelings in my heart again, and it started messing with me, a constant reminder of the painful things I'd been through from the moment I was born.

During the course of my teenage years, my father made sure that we kids experienced different things, like amusement parks, and dude ranches. He wanted us to just have fun. I thought he was a rich man because we seemed to have so much fun all the time. Living with the Crawfords, all I had ever learned was that in life people will hurt you or fail you no matter who they are. They will hurt you because they don't think of anybody but themselves. That stuff still bothered me, but my new father challenged me to reach for something higher for me and my life, which was important in building up my character and my confidence.

Once I graduated from high school, I left home with a quickness. I wanted to experience life, and living under my Mom and Dad's roof that wasn't going to happen.

At first I was employed doing odd jobs, until I found a gig working for the Transportation Department of New Jersey. I was a Bus Operator, which paid pretty good. It's funny how one thinks money is the answer to all of our problems. I thought I would stay on that job forever. But soon I had a change of heart, and decided I wanted to join the Army. I was told not to do that from my family and friends. "Don't join the man's Army," they said. "You won't get anything out of it. Why are you leaving the 'hood? Do you think you are better than us?"

Etc.

Etc.

Yes, I heard it all.

Again I was feeling frustrated, and like the world is a bad place and I didn't want to be in it anymore.

It was a good thing I never gave up. I was fueled by my desire to live my dreams and find my purpose.

I truly believed I'd been given the opportunity because of my bad start in life to make a difference in the lives of others. My rough years as a child had made me stronger, and left me blessed as an adult. I was committed to the next phase of my life shaping me on my journey to find who I really am.

CHAPTER 8:

GIVEN A CHANCE

Over the next few years I channeled that commitment into a direction for my life.

I went from childhood into adulthood. I became a married man, with two young boys. I moved to Orlando, Florida, and joined the Army. I became a Platoon Sergeant, a Drill Sergeant, and an EO Advisor for 5,000 soldiers. I survived harrowing combat missions in Afghanistan, and became a CID Investigator. I intended to fully spend my life working to bring faith, hope and love to those in need.

But somehow, given all that, I knew my journey had just begun.

Somehow, given all I'd accomplished, my head couldn't tune out that same old chatter.

Sure, I'd come a long way, from the shivering baby that was left for dead on somebody's front porch.

But every time I thought about my missing family, it made

my heart stop. It made me think about the real me I was missing.

For me, the yearning to find my family rose from a basic need: I longed to be accepted, after a lifetime of being rejected. That basic yearning for acceptance had been denied to me, from the day I was born. I couldn't bear the idea of me, or anybody, being singled out for neglect and rejection, and not knowing their mother and father, their roots. I'd been shackled to that hurt like a big heavy weight I'd carried around all my life.

I knew that if I didn't deal with that hurt, if I didn't investigate my real beginnings, and find my birth family, all that weight would continue to drag me down, and I would never feel or know real peace.

But how?

Listen:

Throughout my whole life, people had told me, "Kevin, you can't do this" or "Brother, you can't do that."

They told me I wouldn't live because they found me starving on someone's porch...

They told me I wasn't smart enough and that I'd never get a higher education...

They told me the Army wasn't the way to go and I was wasting my time...

They told me I couldn't play sports...

They told me I was too small for martial arts...

They told me, over and over again, that I would fail in life...

And they told me I would never, ever find my bloodline.

I had overcome the impossible, time and time again. My

foster family had been awesome nurturers for me. They always encouraged me. And I felt something inside was encouraging me now, telling me, "You're going to find them, Kevin. Just hang in there. Wait until you get the chance."

But still I felt lost.

And the frustration and the waiting was killing me.

I was 37 years old. I still didn't know who my birth parents were, if I had any brothers or sisters or where they were, and those questions burned a hole inside of me.

It was like I had amnesia, when it came to that. I wanted to know what I was missing. I wanted to know my mother and father's real names. Every person deserves to know that.

I had wandered, like Moses, in the wilderness, on a quest to search for the family I had lost. The family I'd never known. That never knew me. I had never tried looking for my family. But I knew I had to get to a better place, to finally answer that question:

"Who am I, *really?*"

God was giving me a chance, to come out of my shadows.

I couldn't shake that thought out of my mind.

The waiting was over.

No more feeling helpless. No more believing it was impossible. No more letting the past put chains around my future.

And no more living in the shadows.

Now was the time.

PART TWO:

GOING DEEPER
INTO MY SHADOWS

CHAPTER 9:

THE CHASE

As you can tell, I wasn't real good at this waiting part.

All this waiting for *now* had been killing me.

Little did I know that this search for my family would become the turning point in my life. And my main obsession for the next 22 years.

It was 1996, when my wife at the time told me I should start doing the right thing, and track down the birth family that abandoned me.

I was in the military then. Stationed in Germany, Topmpkins Barracks, Schwetzingen, with my wife and my youngest son. My wife was in the military too. We lived off-base in a small town, called Liemen. I was a Squad Leader for the Topo Engineer Company, a Cartographer. That was my job.

Even though the Barnetts had given me a solid foundation for my adult life, they were against me joining the military. Much as I believed a better future lay ahead for me in the military, I was going against the wishes of the family that had helped shape me. So this was like a new chapter beginning in my life.

I also had some major personal issues to battle. I might end up with nothing, after all my searching. Nothing but feeling emotionally and spiritually unwanted all over again.

So heeding the advice of my wife and seeking out my birth family, that was a huge risk—maybe the biggest of my life. I mean, what if I never found them? There were no guarantees that I'd find my mother or father.

At the same time, I was having my fourth child, my youngest child, who'd been born in 1994. So he was 2 years old. And yeah, seeing him burst onto the scene kinda like inspired me to look for my mother, and so when my wife told me the same thing, said, "I want you to find your folks, so my son will know who his grandfather is," I couldn't believe my ears. And I didn't have the heart to refuse her.

So that that was the spark that gave me the motivation, to hire a private detective.

But for a long time I just kept procrastinating. I mean, I was in Germany, in the military, and just didn't know how it could be done.

So what I did was I went on Stars and Stripes, the U.S. military newspaper. They have private investigators listed there, in the classified ads. So I searched through, and picked one.

Before that time I had never tried to track down my parents, or my bloodline. Not once. I would do things like try to search through the database of the state of New Jersey, or go through Vital Statistics, and try to get a copy of my birth certificate. But after years of having no luck, it felt like hiring a private investigator was the way to go.

The investigator was located in Heidelberg. So far, so good. Cost me about $1,500.00. We communicated through the phone and email. I never did meet him in person. I gave him the green light to find my family but the problem was the only information he had to go on was the info I provided from the state.

I told him, based off the information I had, that my last name was Hodge, H-O-D-G-E, and I knew I was born in Jersey City. I knew that my paternal grandfather had passed away in 1946, and so I gave him that information too. I had no information on my mother or my father. Zero.

I did know one other thing.

I knew I had two siblings. Both male. One was two years older and one was 13-14 years older than me. I knew that, because the state of New Jersey can give you what they call "non-identifying information." They give you things like the year you were born, the name of the hospital, stuff like that. They can't give you your mother's name, and they can't give you your mother's birthday, or where your mother has lived before.

Same thing with the siblings. I knew they were out there. But I didn't know anything else.

So basically that's what I had. No names but Hodge. No addresses. I couldn't even get medical records.

So he took that, the private investigator took that, and he ran with it.

I didn't hear from him for awhile. I was getting nervous.

Here I'd bankrolled the man, but I wasn't getting anything back.

Finally I got an email from the detective.

Said he'd narrowed the search for my mother down to a lady, whose phone number he had in New Jersey.

CHAPTER 10:

A SHORT CONVERSATION

I called from my house in Germany. As the phone rang, I started to get worried.

Leading up to that phone call, I'd been very excited, when the private investigator gave me the number of a lady in New Jersey. For the longest time I'd concluded that I wasn't going to find my mother. Now here I was, I had a phone number, I was dialing it, I was excited, and I told my wife yes, *this is it!*

And so I called. And I listened to the phone ring.

Had I thought about any of the things I was going to say to my mother?

Truth is, I just wanted to let her know up front that I wasn't looking for money, or anything like that. I wanted her to know that I turned out to be a very decent individual, a good man, and that I really was only concerned about my medical history, and finding out some information for my children.

So while I'm thinking about my questions, and listening to the phone ring, I'm startled to hear a lady's voice suddenly answer.

"Hello?" she said.

I jumped up, right then. I could feel my skin getting goosebumps.

"Hello," I said back, nervously. Not saying a word for a moment, I just sat and stared at the phone, my heart pounding. "Uh, is this...?" I asked, saying the lady's name.

"Yes it is," the lady answered.

I'm trying to hold back the tears now. I said, "Do you know who this is?"

Her voice was soft. "Yes," she said. Which stunned me. She said, "It's Kevin."

How did she know that? I asked myself. I stared at the phone, not able to ask that question. Finally I said, "Yes, it's Kevin. Kevin Barnett. I'm calling long distance, from Germany. I'm looking for my birth family, and my mother."

"I see," the lady said.

I said, "I'm calling to say I've been good all my life, and I really don't want anything. I just need to know something for my medical records." And then I said, "And I...I think I might be your son."

There was a long stretch of silence. I could feel the tension crawling through the room. I could tell by the silence on the other end that my name, and the fact that I'm calling from overseas, didn't mean anything to her.

"Well," she finally said, and I could tell by the tone of her voice that I wasn't going to like what I was about to hear. But still I could feel myself shivering all over, waiting for her answer.

"Look," she said, "all that's really good, and it's nice to know. But I'm sorry. There's no way I can be your mother."

I stared at the phone. I'm sure my mouth was hanging open and my face was blank. Finally I said, "Really?"

The silence on the other end of the phone lasted forever. I looked down at my hands, and they were shaking. I heard the lady take a deep breath. Then she spoke, and all she said was this:

"Good luck with your search."

And then she hung up.

So that was that. That was a very short conversation.

I put down the phone, not really believing it and not really wanting to. I felt in my heart it was my mother. I don't know if it was just me wanting that feeling. Part of me might not have even minded a lie, at that point.

The woman's voice on the other end sounded calm. Real calm. There was no emotion in her voice. Like nothing I said rattled her. Which I thought was pretty weird, at the time. She was real calm, cool, and collected. I felt like maybe she'd been expecting my call, all these years. Waiting for me to finally find her. Like okay, I'm found, you finally caught me.

Except that it wasn't her.

My mouth felt dry as I heard those words. *There's no way I can be your mother.*

In a flash, everything in my world turned silent and cold.

The first thing that crossed my mind was: *Well, that's the end of that. I'm never gonna find my mom.* Below that layer, in the core of my being, was simple hurt. All those years of abandonment, of being unwanted, a motherless and fatherless child, had been stirred up by this long-awaited phone call, and now it hurt like hell.

At long last, I put the phone down. This wasn't the night I was going to find my mother.

But listen: Did I really think it was my mother?

I thought it was. At the time I thought it was.

I still couldn't fathom in my mind that a woman could know that it was her son calling, and then deny it. I was thinking she was saying no because she had a new life, and didn't want to mess up that new life with the old life. I thought maybe the private investigator had called her up, and tipped her off. Maybe that messed with her mind, and messed everything up.

So I had all these thoughts in my head.

Just hearing the voice I got mad. That voice motivated me. I went back and forth in my imagination with that voice, like maybe it was her, maybe it wasn't. I wrestled with the thoughts in my head.

And so when I called, and it wasn't her, it was a big letdown. It was very disappointing. So it was like I was very high, and then like being on a rollercoaster where your heart stops. So at that point I got very discouraged. I was very down.

I felt unwanted. Again.

I had so much expectation. I became depressed, and angry, and told myself I wasn't going to look for her anymore. I felt so drained, so tapped out, and my thoughts dragged me down further.

So it was a very emotional time.

That cooled me off from looking for my mother for awhile.

So it put it down for about seven years, because I was so discouraged. I couldn't face it.

The next seven years unfolded in a blur. With each passing year, the taste in my mouth for finding my family got sourer and sourer. Until I realized I had one overlooked clue: the name John Hodge.

CHAPTER 11:

"YOU'RE MY SON!"

So I had this lead, this name, John Hodge. The private investigator had found the name, but I'd overlooked it. Maybe because I was so focused on finding my mother.

He also had another name: Gloria Hodge. And a phone number.

But for some reason, I didn't get in touch with her. Not at first.

It was 2003. I'd left Germany, and returned to the States. As I refocused myself on finding my family, the last thing I wanted to try was another cold call. No way. Instead, I got my adopted father, Mr. Barnett, and we went to Lakewood, New Jersey, to go look for this lady.

My father was always someone to whom I could turn for advice. Now that I'd returned home, and found a clue to what I believed was my bloodline, he made sure I wasn't going to give up.

If there was anything that helped me survive all those dehumanizing years of my early childhood, it was my growing up years with the Barnetts. Even after I was a grown man, Mr. Barnett remained a committed father figure to me.

And so together we met up with this lady named Gloria Hodge, at her home, in Red Bank.

And the first thing she said when we met her was, "Yes, yes, oh my god, you're my son, you're my son!"

This lady beamed at me, with a mile-wide smile. That smile was so wide it made me back away, like I was afraid something was gonna jump on me.

And talk about jump: immediately something jumped out at me, when I looked at this lady. When I looked at her, at this Gloria Hodge, she looked nothing like me.

Just as I'm about to say something to my father, Gloria Hodge handed me some photos. In the photos I saw four other kids. None of them looked like me, either. One was supposed to be my bigger brother. There was a sister, and two other brothers. They weren't there, but she told me about them.

She said, "Yeah, I gave up my son, but he wasn't born in 1960, like you claim you were, he was born in 1963, and his last name wasn't Hodge, his last name was Harris." And she was telling me all this stuff, all this information, that didn't sound right.

She said, "You can have these pictures." She placed them in my hand. None of the pictures looked like me. I still have those old photos, somewhere.

My father and me were out of there, a few minutes later.

And after we left, my father said, "What do you think?"

I said, "I don't feel a connection at all."

And he said," I don't feel a connection either."

So we left, both with the same expressions of shock on our faces. But I said to myself: *I'm not leaving until I'm sure this Gloria Hodge is not my mother.*

So we stayed over there in Lakewood for about a day, my father and me. Gloria Hodge arranged for us to meet her children. So I met this so-called brother—anyway, she told me it was my brother—but he didn't look nothing like me.

That meeting just about killed me. I felt another big let-down. Because it seemed like this lady wanted me to be her son. And the only reason I went along with it is because my old foster parent, Mrs. Crawford, told me that my mother's name was Gloria. So that's why that connection right there had me on that wild goose chase.

But even after I left, and went back home, Gloria Hodge never followed up on anything, like she claimed she would. I felt confused, because she was telling me I was gone two years from her life. And she was telling me my name was different. So there was no connection to the facts I knew or anything.

The good thing was I took my adopted father along with me. He told me it's okay, you're gonna find your mother, be patient. "I'm sorry that this happened, son," he said, "I was pulling for you." So that helped me, whereas I felt the whole thing was a big waste of time.

I'd made myself lower my expectations, because of what happened when I called the first woman from Germany. I expected the worst now. I didn't get my hopes up too high. I'd told my Pops, before we met Gloria Hodge, I said, "Listen, if she wants to meet, and if she wants to have a relationship, and it's my mother, then we'll have that." But I also said, "We're going to take a blood test, and we're going to verify everything." I didn't want to be disappointed again.

But we didn't have to go that far. The stuff she said just didn't add up.

So I got sidetracked for awhile again. With the military, with my divorce. Every now and then I'd take out the pictures Gloria Hodge gave me, and I'd stare at them, to see if I could see some kind of resemblance. But there was none. So I kind of put it on a back burner, because it wasn't a high priority, because I had school to study for, a whole lotta things going on, and I didn't have any time to search.

The only time I started thinking about it was when I did my yearly physical, and having the doctors ask me questions. Stuff like, do I have a family history of cancer? Or heart problems? And of course I wouldn't know. So I'd start thinking about it again.

And checking Vital Statistics again.

Calling up the state again.

Giving up again.

I did learn one thing from the lady.

I found this out through the investigator too. I had a bloodline through Trinidad. So that gave me some type of identity, that I was from the Caribbean, that either my mother or my father's side was from that part of the world. So I held onto that information for a long time.

After that, I tried to call Gloria Hodge, one more time. But I didn't get any answer. The phone just rang and rang. So that was enough for me.

But that was the start of the chase.

CHAPTER 12:

CAN'T STRAIN
MY BRAIN

My second son, Isaiah, was the one who got me started on the hunt again.

He said, "Dad, are you gonna keep looking, to find your family?"

I must've gritted my teeth when I heard that question. I answered him as truthfully as I could. "Son," I said, "you know it will be difficult to find them. After all, it's been 46 years."

I could see he was unimpressed with my excuse. To me, it was like I can't keep wasting my life, I can't strain my brain anymore with this. But he had this dogged determination that I was gonna find out my family history. And he had this look in his little eyes that said to me, *All right, Pop, I'm counting on you. You can do this.*

So that kind of like motivated me to do it again.

Soon I was embroiled again in the search.

The only person in my family I told about my search was my adopted father. He was the only one who knew about it, and my siblings in the Barnetts. It wasn't a secret, but I didn't flaunt it out there. I expressed to them my uneasiness, and that it would be too painful for me to fail again.

So I called the state again. This was in 2006. And the state told me to put myself in this database. The state's genealogical history records database, which was one of the largest collections of family history records on the web, and which was searchable.

So I put myself in this database. Soon as I did that, the state sent a letter to my birth mom, letting her know I was in the database. The letter also said I wanted to get in touch with her, for medical reasons.

They came back to me pretty quick. And they said that they know my mother is still alive, but she had no desire to contact me.

Once again, I'm angry. I'm a little bit older, but I'm angry, knowing that she's alive and still rejecting me.

So here we go with another rejection. Now I'm going back in my head: okay you rejected me when I was born, now you've rejected me two or three times since then, now here I am 46 years old, and you're still rejecting me. What possibly have I done? Why don't you want to see me?

In one part of my brain, I was glad I'd found out that my mother was alive. And in the other part there was this sadness that she didn't want to have contact with me.

Well, I thought, *that's the same feeling she had when I was born.* So I was sad, I was angry, a little bit, so I just did things like to go school, try to get my degree, all kinds of things to keep my mind off it. I wanted to do all these great things, that she'd be proud of. That was the driving force, in everything I did.

I had anger for a long time, being shut down. Being shut off. Being turned away. It affected my relationship with my wife, which suffered. And it affected my relationship with my boys too. I wasn't close to them, like I should have been. And so it caused a lot of problems. But I didn't blame my mom. It was more like it put a light on me to be all that I could be, in anything I did, just to prove to her that she missed out. So that's how I dealt with my anger. I knew that she was getting older, and the fact that she held onto those old feelings, and probably knowing that I'd come close to finding her, because I lived in New Jersey, she knew that I knew that she was alive.

So rejection was really hard.

When she rejected me, it took me right back to Miss Crawford, how she used to say things like your mother don't like you, she doesn't want you. So now I'm asking myself: is this true? Why would a lady not want her son? A son and mother relationship should be really close. So why doesn't she want me? What did I do?

I never even gave it a thought that there was a good reason why she did it. It bothered me at times, when my adopted family would look at home movies, and things like that, and prior to 1970 I wasn't in them. That brought up these feelings too. We'd have a family gathering, they'd be showing home movies that I wasn't a part of. I never saw no pictures of me as a little baby. I didn't know how much I weighed when I was born. I didn't know how many inches long I was. I didn't know any of these things. So that brought anger, from a different perspective.

Yeah. So it wasn't good, being rejected. I remembered when I was back in the military, when I went out to clubs in Germany, it kind of affected me with how I interacted with the opposite sex. I wanted to make sure a girl liked me, before I actually went out with her. So I used to play games, and make sure I was making the right moves with the young ladies, because I didn't want to feel that feeling of rejection.

I didn't want to fail at anything. All of my feelings stemmed from that. So whatever I did, I told myself I gotta push through, no matter how hard it is, because I don't want to fail. Because then I'm just bringing on whatever prophecy that Mrs. Crawford was laying on me.

Stuff like, *I told you you'd fail.* Stuff like, *I told you you wasn't any good.*

But I used all of that rejection, to make me stronger. And a better man.

I could have given up so many times. Look how many times I could've given up! But something in my heart kept pushing me. It was more than just finding my mother. I knew I had siblings, that I wanted to meet. So I never gave up. I never surrendered.

So now I was totally motivated. Like, *I know you're out there. I know you're alive. And I'm gonna find you. Sooner or later, I'm gonna find you.*

CHAPTER 13:

GOING IN CIRCLES

Fast forward…

It's a few years later. 2011.

I called the state again. Looking for my mother. Hoping she'd tried to get in contact with me. And the state gave me the same answer. "Your mother doesn't want any contact with you."

I was 51 now. I'd been going on 14, 15 years now with this hunt. Mathematically-wise, I'm thinking she must be up there in age. She's probably not gonna make it, and I'm not going to find her before she passes away.

I wanted to give up, but I was motivated to find out something about myself, to come out of my shadows, whether it was me finding my mother or me finding my siblings. So I gave up to the point where I wasn't going to call the state anymore. They hadn't given me any more information than I already knew.

I thought there might be some other way to find my siblings, and not bother with finding my mother.

I was doing a lot of travelling for my job. I was married for the third time, so I was trying to put more time in my marriage. So my priorities shifted a bit. I became a grandfather, things like that. So while finding my family was important, it wasn't on the top of my list anymore.

It wasn't until 2013, when I called the state again. And that's when I talked to a different lady at the state, and I said, "Listen, I want to get my medical records. I have grandkids. I need to know my history."

Stuff like that.

But they gave me the same answer again. "Your mother doesn't want any contact with you."

The first time I'd heard that, I was stunned by the intensity of my feelings. Now I felt like I'm going in circles. Once again, here I was, thinking after hunting down all this information I was close to finding my mother. I'd get pumped up and the adrenaline would be flowing. I could feel it, taste it, touch it— there was no way I could miss, not a second time, not a third time! Then I'd get hit by the same jolt of rejection that hit me the first time, only harder, and my instinctual reaction, just like before, was: *Oh yeah, this is impossible. It's never gonna happen.*

But not giving up were the watchwords for my life.

So I called the state up again in 2014. And this time I told the lady at the state, "Listen, it's very imperative to find my mother, and to talk to her, because, you know, I have different things going on with me, like bad headaches and stuff. So I want to make sure that it not anything hereditary or anything like that."

It's true, I was getting migraines. These migraine headaches. Part of it was from being deployed in Afghanistan, but I also used to get headaches a lot when I was growing up, because of the malnutrition. And these headaches were scaring me. I had to take time off from work. I lost time with my family. So I thought to myself, maybe it's something hereditary. I needed some answers.

The lady listened to me. She said she'd try contacting my mom again.

But they came back with the same answer again.

So that did it. It finally dawned on me that I was back to going in circles. So I ended up hiring another private investigator. This was in the early part of 2016. Whereas the first investigator was based in Germany, this one was in Delaware.

I gave the investigator this new piece of information the state had given me. The last time I'd called the lady told me this. She said, "Listen, because of our rules you know I can't tell you the private information you need. But I can tell you this much. Your grandmother passed away in Virginia."

So I did some research. I found the only person who had the last name of Hodge who passed away on the date they gave me. So I took that information, and gave it to the private investigator.

And that's when I really started going at it hard. So I hired him, and he found me the name of Minnie Hodge. He also found some information on the kids and stuff like that.

But then he hit a dead end. All the paths he was following dried up.

But I knew I was too close to stop now. So I started checking into these family history and family ancestry websites.

I joined AncestryDNA.com.

Also joined 23andme.

And FamilyTreeDNA.

And GEDMatch.

I joined up with a whole lotta sites, everywhere and everything I could find. And at the same time, I took a DNA test. Then I joined some groups on Facebook that dealt with adoption. People looking for their parents and stuff.

That led me to get on Facebook, based on some information I had found on some blood cousins from Ancestry.com. They told me about two groups on Facebook, the Search Angels and the DNA Detectives.

And so through those two groups, I took the information that I had. And I followed it. Hard. And for months, I just went down a rabbit hole. Everywhere I could, on every website, I'd post a message. I also sent a letter to the cousins I found on AncestryDNA:

Hello,

I am an adoptee that is looking for my birth parents and 2 older brothers. My birth name was Kevin Hodge, born July 30 1960 at Jersey City Memorial Hospital in New Jersey. I have no information on any of my brothers or birth parents. It's a possibility that my birth Grandmother's name is Minnie E. Hodge who passed away on February 2, 1998 in Norfolk, Virginia.

I sent another letter to a potential cousin I found on Ancestry, based on the first info I received from the state of New Jersey:

Hello,

I'm looking for my biological relatives. I was adopted in 1970 and was in the foster care program since 1960 which is the year I was born. I just completed my DNA test and results match with you (4th-6th cousin). If interested I would like to chat with you.

Kev

And then I waited.

Waiting was bad enough. But when it came to getting replies that didn't match up, that was the worst. Everything I came up with was totally off.

But that marked another turning point for me.

It turned out I had a Search Angel on my side.

And *bam!* That angel started the ball rolling.

CHAPTER 14:

MY ANGEL

They call 'em "search angels" in the genealogy community. They're the folks who volunteer their time and talents to guide lost children like me in the hunt for their biological families.

Never met my angel in person. Just talking through Facebook.

We exchanged a bunch of information. Trying to narrow down the results she found and find a match for my family.

And unfortunately we came to a dead end. Turns out the information that the private detective gave me was wrong, it couldn't be true, because things didn't match up.

That's when I called the state again in the summer, and they told me that whoever told you the previous info about your birth family was wrong.

So I gave that new info to the angel, and she came up with a match: *Oh,* she wrote me, *your mother's name is this, she had two kids, one kid had two kids, that has to be your mother.* So she started finding everything.

So I called the agency one more last time, in June of 2016, and I said, "Listen, I know I am probably gonna get the same answer, but I am just checking to see if my mother is in the database."

And they said *No.*

I said "Well, at least I think I know where my grandmother is at." And I gave them the information on her.

And then as if in answer to prayers I hadn't even prayed yet, a miracle happened. Right there on the telephone.

See, this was a whole different lady at the state this time. And she said, "Wait a minute. Who is your grandmother?"

I said, "My grandmother is Minnie Hodge, and she was born in 1800 and something in the state of Virginia and she died in 1996."

And the lady said, "Whoever told you that was wrong."

I said, "Hmmm…" I almost let out an audible sigh, when she said that. I'm thinking, *Damn, here we go again.* And I'm overflowing with suspicion.

The lady said, "Since she passed away, I can't tell you her name, but I can tell you that your grandmother was born in Templeton, Virginia, and she passed away in Asbury Park, New Jersey in 1996."

Her words were the equivalent of a thunderclap, a lightning bolt, striking me.

I almost got used to the answers they state would give me. I'd be calling, almost out of routine, knowing I'd get the same answer.

And here this state lady was, she took that risk, that small miracle in my favor, and made an even bigger miracle in my heart. And that kept me going, when I was about ready to throw up my hands and say, I give up, I'm never gonna find my siblings, I'm never gonna talk to my mom.

And so now all these puzzle pieces started falling into place. All the loose ends I'd had were beginning to tie together.

At the same time, the state of New Jersey was changing the laws, about birth certificates. In 2017 the state was gonna give persons who'd been given up for adoption access to their birth records. So if I didn't find out before then, I knew I'd be able to get a birth certificate, which would have had her name on there. Then—BOOM!—I'd have her.

So I took that information, that the lady from the state gave me, and I started running with it, to see if I could find out any more information from it. Because now somebody had told me something that was totally different.

You see, Asbury Park wasn't where I thought my mother was at. I thought my mother was in Bricktown, New Jersey. Or Lakewood, New Jersey.

Mind you, I had nothing on my father so far, so I was strictly sticking to my mother's side.

And so I got on the Internet, on DNA Detectives. And what happens is you have to put your story on there. Tell folks what happened to you, why you got adopted, what you know about your birth family, stuff like that.

I also put on my non-identifying information on the site.

And then I waited.

It was hard, because I had nothing to go on. I mean *nothing*.

I couldn't even imagine anymore what my birth family looked like, except from what I looked like. So I'd imagine my brother is the same height as me, the same color as me, same hair as me. I had no image of anybody. I didn't know if my mother was short, tall, fat, skinny. I had no way of knowing anything about her, except that when I was a kid I figured she was mean, because she left me. That was the only thing I had.

I had such a poor perception of my mother, because of how she gave me up for adoption.

Having to puzzle out and compartmentalize all that stuff and keep it contained was always beating me down. The weight of the stress and fear I was carrying from all the searches I'd run started getting heavy. I started to get the sinking feeling that my vision of meeting my birth family was never going to happen. I started having sleeping problems again. It's like my brain was becoming a combat zone. When I finally did give in to sleep at night I didn't dream at all, just listened to the unconscious questions ramming my brain:

Who am I?

Am I ever going to know the answer?

Why doesn't anybody want me?

Meanwhile I waited. And waited.

And all that waiting put me back in my shadows, with this unbearable weight pressing down on my shoulders and around my heart, and no place to hide.

Then one night, I'll never forget it. It was like, *whoooo!* I went on one of the sites, and I put on there that I hadn't yet found my parents, and I was about to give up, stuff like that. A totally hopeless message. Because sometimes it seems like there is no hope. Sometimes you just sit there, waiting for somebody to write back.

But nobody does.

Not that night.

CHAPTER 15:

NEVER GONNA
GIVE YOU UP

Someone saw it. The message I'd posted.

And they wrote me back, and said, *Let me see if I can help you.*

Just like that. *Let me see if I can help you.* I had to steady myself from falling over, when I read those words.

She asked, *Where was you born?*

I gave her the non-identifying information. The same stuff I'd been carrying around with me for years.

And she started typing.

Type, type, type.

I think I found something, she wrote.

My throat went tight. I swallowed hard.

What? I wrote back.

There was a pause. Then she started typing again.

Type, type, type.

I think your grandmother's name is Cora Hodge, she wrote.

And I said to myself, *Oh, really?* This angel obviously knew all the tricks, the loopholes, to getting confidential information the other angels hadn't found.

It was so quiet in the house that I could hear my own heartbeat. A second later, my angel wrote back:

Let me try something else.

Type, type, type.

She had two daughters, she wrote me.

At first I didn't believe it. I couldn't. I wasn't sure how to react. What she had found matched up with the non-identifying information I had. I had a mom, that only had one sister.

So then she gave me some more information.

She wrote, *Let's see which one had kids.*

Type, type, type.

She said, *Oh, looks like this one had kids, and she had two kids.*

I wrote, *How old are they?*

One is three years older than you, she wrote, *and one is 14 years older than you.*

So right then I got scared. My heart started bumpin', and beepin', and I felt my old feelings pounding away at me—the cruel words Mrs. Crawford told me, that I was worthless and would always be worthless and unwanted. All those nights I cried myself to sleep asking God why—*why* I had to live with the Crawfords, *why* I couldn't live with my parents, *why* it was taking so long for them to come find me.

I breathed hard. My mind assuring me that this new

information might be true.

And then disaster struck.

The angel told me, *Her father passed away in 1946.*

I looked at the screen. Disappointment overflowing. I felt my mind plunging back into despair.

And I wrote, *Wait a minute, on the records it said that it was my paternal father who passed away.*

She typed, *They probably got that part wrong. It was your maternal father who passed away in 1946, and your brother was born in 1947.*

And she kept typing away. And then she said, *Oh by the way, one of your brothers passed away, and you also have a sister.* Which at that point that was totally news to me. She said, *And they live in Asbury Park,* and she showed me the house and everything.

Soon as my angel showed me that my old anguish began to drift away. The answers to all my prayers and my problems were right in front of me.

So what I did after that, I went online to this place called White Pages, Premium White Pages, and I started looking. I started hunting. And I started getting phone numbers, right? I got some numbers, and one of them was the phone number to my mother's house, and I called the number.

And when I called the number, a young lady answered the phone. And said hello.

CHAPTER 16:

DESPERATE MEASURES

I was nervous. I held the phone in my sweaty fingers. And finally I said "Hello" back.

"Yes, can I help you?" the young lady said back.

And I said, "Yes, I want to speak to Ms. Hodge."

And she said, "Well why would you want to speak to her?"

Oh Lord. What could I say? I couldn't avoid the question.

And I said, "Well, I think I'm a relative."

Silence.

She said, "Well what do you mean you think you're a relative?"

I let my breath out carefully. I leaned my mouth in close to the phone, and I said, I just told her, "Well, I believe I'm your son."

And she said, "Whoa, no, wait a minute. There's no way in the world you're my son."

I lifted my ear away from the phone. Now here's what I

didn't know at that moment: this was not my mother on the phone. This was my *sister* on the phone. And she was protecting my mother, on account of she thought I was a bill collector.

So she said back to me, "Look now, listen, I don't have time to play games, you have a nice day." And she hung up the phone.

Click!

So now I'm in a state of disbelief. I'm saying to myself, well, I already blew that! I wasn't prepared or nothing. I wasn't prepared for anybody to answer the phone. Especially not my sister! I assumed if somebody did answer the phone, it would be my mom. The voice on the other end of the phone had shut me down good.

So at this time I had to do some thinking. Finally I came up with a desperate measure.

Around this time I had a business trip to take to Colorado. And so I said to myself, I'm gonna try this again. This time, I'm gonna call my brother. 'Cuz I'd finally found my brother's phone number. It was dangerous, I knew, but it was also thrilling at the same time to know I was so close. And I wasn't powerless.

So I got myself together, and I kinda like wrote down some notes of what I need to do, you know, when I call my brother.

The number I had was in his wife's name. So I called the phone number, and listened to it ring and ring. Finally she answered the phone.

And I said, "Hello, can I speak to Velma?" Velma, that's her name.

Immediately things took a turn for the worse.

She said, "Velma's not home."

Now I knew that was her, it was Velma, that answered the phone. So I'm saying to myself, *Okay, this ain't going well.* A sick feeling of dread came into my stomach.

She said. "Can I take a message for Velma?"

Where to begin? I thought. I didn't know, so I decided to forge on.

I said "Yes," changing up the subject, "I'm trying to get in touch with Johnny Hodge." Johnny Hodge was the name of my brother. The words choked out of me, my voice probably giving away my nerves.

To my surprise and my shock, she didn't hang up. I didn't hear the click like I did the first time. She didn't even sound skeptical.

She said, "Oh, hold on. He's here."

CHAPTER 17:

TRACKING

He's here?

I bit my lower lip, waiting to see if he came on the phone. And I heard somebody in the background saying, "There's somebody on the phone looking for you that called for me, and I told 'em I wasn't there, but then they asked for you, and it sounds very important."

And then I heard my brother say, "Okay."

And so he got on the phone, and as he got on the phone I felt this heat rising inside of me.

I said, "So how you doin' John?"

In my mind's eye, I'm seeing him on the other end of the phone, wondering *Who the hell is this? A damn bill collector tracking me down?*

The irony is: he was halfway right. I might not have been a bill collector. But I had spent more than fifty years of my life tracking him down.

"First of all," I said, "I want you to know that I'm not a bill collector, and I'm not looking for any money or anything else. I'm just gonna take 10 minutes of your time, and it's very important. It's about your family, and I'm gonna tell you the whole nine yards if you'll let me."

I stood still and felt my eyes filling with tears as I waited to hear his reaction.

He said, "Okaaay."

I said, "Are you sittin' down?"

I could hear his voice drop. He said, "You're scaring me now."

I said, "I don't wanna scare you. I'm just gonna let you know something."

"Okaaay," he repeated.

I told him, "Your mother's name is Cora Hodge." My voice became gentle, my words careful.

"Okay," he repeated back.

I said, "And your grandfather's name is Thomas Hodge."

He said, "Mmmm-hmmm."

I said, "Thomas Hodge came over to the United States from St. Kitts around 1908. He caught a ship, and he sailed, and it dropped him off in Manhattan, and from there he ended up meeting a young lady named Cora Taylor. They wound up getting married, she became Cora Hodge, and ended up migrating down to Asbury Park. They had two kids. Two girls. Are we still okay?"

"Mmmm-hmmm," he said.

"And one daughter had two kids, one named Kenny, one named Johnny. And the other daughter had a kid by the name of Delores."

And he said, "Mmm-hmmm."

I said, "Is this kinda tracking right now?" That's an Army term, *tracking*.

And he said, "Yes."

I said, "Cora Hodge, your grandmother, passed away in 1996, and Kenny passed away in the 1990s sometime. And your grandfather, Thomas Hodge, passed away in 1946. Am I tracking?"

And he said, "Mmm-hmmm."

I said, "Okay." And I took a deep breath, and tried to imagine what my brother was thinking. I said, "I wanted to tell you all of this to tell you this. My name is Kevin. My birth name is Kevin Hodge, okay? I was born in 1960 in a maternity room in Jersey City. I have four boys, I've been in the military twenty years and I'm retired. The day I was born my birth mother gave me up for adoption. I've been through the court foster care system and wound up finding a home and I was given the name Kevin Barnett, and ever since I've known that I was not a Barnett I've been looking for my parents, and I want to let you know that I am your brother." I waited, listening to my brother breathe on the other end of the phone, wondering if he was going to say anything. But he stayed silent. I said, "I tried to call Mrs. Bean, because she married, but I believe my sister Anna answered the phone, and in her haste she was protecting my mother, so I didn't have time to explain to her. So now I'm calling you, to see if you can contact them."

There was a long sigh, on the other end of the phone.

I said, "I'll be going through Colorado on a business trip,

and this is my phone number. But I wanted to present that to you, to give you a chance to digest that, and maybe pass that information on to Ms. Hodge."

Never before had I gotten the chance to say those words to anybody. Before, my nerves would have talked me out of it. But when I finally said them, I felt a sense of peace surge through me.

I heard my brother take another deep breath. And then he said, "Wow."

He said, "I'll take your number, and I'll get back with you."

So then he hung the phone up.

In the blink of an eye, the moment I'd waited for all my life had come and gone. And my greatest fears had not come to pass. My brother had not rejected me. And now there was a chance that my mother, who had disappeared more than fifty years ago, would reach out and contact me.

So in the meanwhile, after my brother hung up, I was still kinda upset—mostly because I didn't handle the first phone call right. So I went ahead and I wrote a letter.

I wrote a letter telling my mother who I was, my name is Kevin Barnett, blah blah blah, and then I put a picture of me with four of the Caribbean flags. St. Kitts, Bahamas, Trinidad, and the Virgin Islands, and I put the picture of me profiling. And I put that picture as part of the letter, and I sealed it up, and I knew the address to send it to, so I sent it to my Mom, in Asbury:

> Hello Ms. Hodge Bean,
> I am writing this letter because I don't have the words

yet to talk in person. I believe I am closely related to you. My name is Kevin Hodge, born 1960. Through my investigations and taking DNA testing I found out that I have a brother named John Hodge, Thomas Hodge and a sister named Annie Bean. I believe my grandfather name is Thomas Hodge and he came from the West Indies St. Kitts. This info leads me to believe that you are my birth mother.

I understand the circumstances that surrounded the reason why I was put up for adoption and have no hard feelings. I just wanted to touch bases with you to confirm these findings. I'm not looking for anything other than closure. I would like to know my blood relatives' medical history and info that will help me and my children later on in life.

To let you know I have 4 young men 33, 28, 26, and 22. I have 5 grandchildren as well. I graduated from High School in 1979 and worked with the Transportation of New Jersey as a Bus Operator. I later joined the Military Service and was stationed in Germany for about 9 years. I stayed in the Army and retired after over 20 years of service. During my time in the service I obtained a AA, BS and MS degrees.

During my spare time I have participated in the Martial Arts from which I received a 2nd Degree Black Belt in Hapkido. I also played Football and Basketball while in the service.

I am currently happily married and have a Stepdaughter. I have nothing to complain about because life has been very good to me. I just wanted to thank you and hopefully I can meet your sister Veronica (Aunt) and my siblings Annie and John.

I sincerely hope I didn't cause any problems with the phone call and I wish in my heart we can meet. My contact number is listed below if you decide to want to chat. Take care and God Bless.

Kevin Hodge

And then I got on the plane, and I went to Colorado. On my business trip. And that first night I had trouble sleeping. It's funny how long the nights are, when your imagination is running wild.

Now the second day in Colorado—and remember, I told my brother I wasn't going to contact them until I got back from the business trip—but for some reason, I just couldn't hold on. So after the second day on the business trip I ended up calling John.

The number rang a couple of times. Then John answered. Soon as I heard his voice, I was shaking all over.

I said, "Hey, how you doin' John?" I said, "Was you able to pass on that information?"

He said, "Yeah."

"So what did she say?" I asked.

He said, "She didn't deny anything."

I said, "Huh." *Well, thank God for that,* I thought. I said, "When I get back, I'll probably give you a call again. I'm very happy."

He said, "I'm happy too. And I can't wait to meet you."

So we hung up the phone. And I walked back and forth around my hotel room, exploding with good news, and without a single ear to hear it.

In the meanwhile, I sent a text to Anna, my sister, 'cuz I found out what her cell number was. In the text I wrote: *do you know who this is?*

And she texted me back and said: *yes I do.*

I said *who is it?*

She said *it's my brother.*

Those three words just about crushed my heart to dust. The smile I felt break out on my face must've been as wide as the sky. I felt certain my sister wouldn't want me prying into her situation. The terrible part was that I still had questions about everything: my mother, my father, why they abandoned me. But I was beginning to tune out my confused, fearful feelings. And I just wasn't going to listen to my worries about being rejected anymore.

So I called my sister up. And me and Anna just clicked. Just like that. And so she said, "Well I can't wait to meet you."

Boom boom boom, went my heart.

So I started to have these conversations with Anna. And I talked to my brother Johnny over the phone, we was talking back and forth, back and forth, like we'd grown up together all our lives, and yet all this time I knew something was still missing.

As good as it felt to talking to my siblings, I knew that this chapter in the story wasn't the end, there was another chapter that needed to be written.

I knew we had to take the next step.

I said, "Listen, we gotta meet. We need to find a place. I need to meet my Mom."

PART THREE:

EXITING MY SHADOWS

CHAPTER 18:

SEPTEMBER 17, 2016

I said, "Listen, we gotta meet. We need to find a place. But where?"

So I have a friend I went to high school with. He owns a restaurant in Asbury Park, called At The Table. It's a soul food restaurant, a really laid-back, family-run joint featuring home-style Southern cooking.

So I got on the phone with him, and we started talking, and he said he was totally on-board with my plan. Then the next thing he said was, "Hey listen, I know this sounds weird. But I know someone named Johnny Hodge. My wife used to go to work in a carpool with him."

"Really?" I said.

So I talked with his wife, she said yeah, me and Johnny Hodge carpooled for about 14-15 years,

Again, all these connections were becoming over whelming.

So I called up my brother Johnny. He said, "Yes, I know her."

That's crazy, right? But nothing about my hunt surprised me anymore. I said, "Okay, well this is where we're gonna have the get-together for the first time, we're gonna have it at this restaurant, called At The Table. You know it?"

"Yeah," Johnny said.

"I told my friend it's gonna be about 16 people," I said.

So I got Anna and John's help in organizing everything. We set a date: Saturday, September 17, 2016.

Next thing I know, it's September 17, I'm driving with my wife in her Nissan Murano to the restaurant.

Well it was a long drive. An hour and a half. It felt like the longest drive of my life. I was anxious, nervous, didn't know what I was gonna say. I'm meeting my birth mother for the first time. Was she going to accept me? I know I'd spoken to her over the phone, I'd even Facetimed her, so I felt comfortable that she was going to accept me and everything. Still, I was nervous. Would she hug me? What would she look like in person? How tall is she? Did she really remember me? Will she stare at me? Will I stare at her?

So yeah, I was nervous. I drove, and my stepdaughter and my wife came with me. We listened to music and chit-chatted and had whole conversations and stuff, though never about the meeting. We never talked about it until we got closer. Then the closer and closer we got, the more I started to question was this a good idea? They were asking me was I nervous? Was I scared? Told me just to be myself, and that this is what I'd been waiting for.

I didn't think too much about meeting my brother and sister either, because I'd talked to them a lot on the phone, and I'd Facetimed my sister. But I was nervous about meeting them in person, hugging them and touching them. My Mom was the main one, though, the number one priority.

We pull into Asbury Park. Right up to At The Table. And just like that we're at this soul food restaurant, waiting for everybody to arrive, and my step-daughter she's a photographer, so she jumps inside, sets the table just right, getting all the angles and all that.

And that's when I seen them walking up the street to the restaurant.

So now I'm getting nervous and everything.

It's 50-plus years I'm building up for this moment, right?

Sure enough, as I step over to the door, there she comes walking in. My Mom. More beautiful than I ever could have imagined.

She was short—about four foot six—with dark skin like myself. Looked like her eyes were hazel. Her hair was black and silky. And I could tell right away, she had a hell of a sense of humor.

Between my shock and my euphoria, I don't know what to say.

The minute they walked in, I'm drowned in tears and with a big lump in my throat. My eyes welled up with the knowledge that for the first time I was looking at my mother. The woman who gave birth to me. With her arms open wide to me.

She stopped in the door. Crying. Looking at me. She had like this amazing smile, and we looked at each other, and we hugged. And so I backed off, 'cuz I could see she was getting ready to cry some more.

I said, "Don't cry," and we both got choked up and just stared at each other. As we stood side-by-side, hugging each other again, I realized how short my mother was.

I'm holding her, I'm hugging her tight to me, still not realizing what's happening. Until slowly it dawns on me that *this is real*.

Excitedly, my Mom turned and gestured towards the rest of the family.

So I let her go, and I hugged my Aunt Ronnie, and her sister, and then my cousin Delores who'd been diagnosed with cancer, everybody telling me she actually sacrificed a lot to come see me, and here's her daughter come to see me too. And then of course I finally met my brother Johnny, and my sister Anna.

The next surprise was that another relative of mine decided to show up, unannounced.

Seems there was this guy named Larry, who was walking by the restaurant, and he looked in there, saw his family inside, and so he came in. And I didn't know who he was, come to find Larry's a cousin too!

He said, "What's going on?"

Everybody said, "We come to meet Kevin."

And Larry just stared. Hit everybody with one of those furrowed-brow expressions.

He said, "Who's Kevin?"

"He's your aunt's son."

"My aunt's son? Kevin?"

"Yeah! They're reuniting."

"Reuniting?"

"Yeah!"

And so now *he's* hugging everybody!

Listening to all these conversations about me, I tried my best not to be rattled. I have to admit, it was bizarre. All of a sudden, everybody wants to know where I live, where I work, what I've been doing all my life. Fifty years and nobody's been keeping tabs on me and now after worrying I'd have to pass some kinda test or something to join the family, and I didn't have to prove a damn thing.

My waiting was over.

So when I managed to pull myself out of the blur of space and pull myself back to reality we sat down to eat. For two hours we ate pulled chicken and swapped family stories and just laughed and talked. Although the truth is my stomach was tight and eating was not my main concern.

My Mom had the fried chicken platter, yams, and collared greens. I had the same thing, barely touching a bite. My sister, she'd been to this place before, and it seems like when she'd been there they never had the pulled chicken, so I made sure that my friend had it for her. They had a bunch of pulled chicken in little hamburger buns for her.

I had this Army book, that I brought as a conversation piece, in case things got awkward, talked about me being in Afghanistan and stuff, things I did in the military.

And so my mother sat on one side, my brother sat on the other side, I sat at the head of the table, and we flipped through that Army book and talked and laughed. My Mom kept on staring at me, and I was staring at her. The sight of everybody seated together at one table made me catch my breath.

My sister Anna was staring at me too, taking pictures, because she said I looked exactly like my brother Kenny who passed away. And my mother stared at me a whole lot.

Oh, and she winked at me a couple of times.

Or maybe that's what I'm thinking.

Anyway, we hung out and everybody heard the story of my life and we laughed. Everyone was smiling and hospitable, and treated me like a celebrity. The more we hung out, and the family stories started to roll, the fewer differences I saw between us. And there were aspects of myself I could see had come from my mother's side of the family.

And to my wife and my step-daughter, these people who'd walked in her as strangers were their family now.

There were a few other people in the restaurant. They kinda asked what was going on, and we told them and they said, "Oh, that's so nice!" Some of them clapped when my mother came through and I hugged my mother.

We had good conversations for about two hours, took some pictures outside, and then my brother John went around the corner to get his car, and he let loose a little bit.

I looked up and saw Johnny was crying.

I told him not to cry, everything's OK. He hugged me about four or five times. John's the oldest one. He said he remembered when my mother was pregnant with me, said he knew she disappeared for about three months and then came back. So he had a feeling what happened, but he couldn't really pinpoint it. He was the only man in the family for a long time, until Kenny was born, so he felt a lot of relief knowing he had another brother out there now.

So we took pictures, and then we went over to John's house, and we took more pictures. I met my brother's wife. Larry's wife came through. We just stayed there another two hours, talking about the whole scenario, how I found them and the whole nine yards. They showed me some pictures of Kenny and some of the family events I'd missed.

The whole time, all these happy feelings swirled up inside of me. My accomplishments in the military and as a man had obviously made my Mom proud. Everybody I looked at that day had a big smile on their face. In an instant my world turned inside out.

Only after looking as deeply as I had into my mother's eyes was I able to fully understand the reasons she gave me up all those lonesome years ago. And I understood now why my being unwanted had led to my being raised by the Barnetts, who planted the belief in me that I could do whatever in life I dreamed of doing, and that became the secret to my success that followed.

Afterwards, when we were driving home, I cried. I won't lie to you. I shed some more tears when I was by myself in the bathroom. For a long while I'd been afraid that words might shatter the magic of this moment. The spell that meeting my Mom cast over the day obliterated all the pain from before.

I felt incredibly lucky to be able to give all the love I'd been deprived of during my childhood at the Crawfords to my real birth family. Nothing would dampen that memory, as long as I live. After living a life of secrets, a life of hard times and never hearing anything about my mother, my father or my siblings, I was feeling like we all might live happily ever after.

September 17th became a moment I could return to and visit in my mind anytime I wanted to. Unlike many of the painful experiences of my childhood that tended to blur and fade away, this moment became a vivid reality that my mind latched onto in perfectly preserved detail.

It was one of the most awesome days of my life. For the rest of my life, there will never be another moment like that. It's on the top of that list, the top of that mountain.

CHAPTER 19:

THE FUNERAL

And so in a nutshell that's basically how I met my mother.

But my celebration was short-lived. Before I could figure out my next move, I was invited to a family funeral.

My cousin Delores—the one I'd met who'd been diagnosed with cancer—she passed away soon thereafter.

Delores called me on a Monday, right after we met. Told me she was glad she met me, that she loved me. I tried to call her again, but I didn't get any answer. Then the next day she passed away. So right away, I had to go to a funeral. And so that was another big family event. Everything was moving at a breakneck pace and everybody I met from that moment on was all brand new to me.

I never thought about the time with my new family members being limited. Now that I'd found my birth family, the last thing on my mind was losing one of them.

So now I go to a funeral. It was in a church, in Asbury Park.

With a combination of nerves and excitement, I'm driving to the funeral. And now the family members that I never seen before in my life, from Connecticut and from Asbury, all around the East Coast and from all from my mother's side of the family, they all came to the funeral. And I'm like, *wow!*

Cars were parked up and down both sides of the street. It seemed like the world had stopped because this one person was gone. Of course, there was crying and comforting and people coming in from out of town, everybody talking about how at least Delores' suffering and misery were over. I knew all the tears were because my cousin Delores was so well loved.

And of course everybody's telling me I look like my brother Kenny, and talking about me finding my Mom, and stuff like that. I met a cousin who lived not even ten minutes away from me, in Delaware. We met up in Maryland for the very first time, her last name is Shorter.

So I met Hodges, I met Shorters, and I met Taylors, all on my mother's side.

The feeling of elation I got every time I met a new member of my family never diminished. That feeling erased all doubt in my mind that finding my family had been worth all the pain I experienced. All the worries, the anxieties, the doubts...everything was going to be fine. It was like all that stuff had been plucked right out of my life.

So for me, the day was a lot like a funeral mixed with a reunion. I met more relatives. After the funeral was over with, we went straight to a Mason Hall, and there I met more new people. More new faces. My brother and sister introduced me to a ton of my cousins. So it was an awesome day, and a very sad day.

I had all the pain and grief mixed with all these new faces coming around to meet me. And now that it was behind me, I still had one more goal lying ahead.

CHAPTER 20:

FINDING MY FATHER

Now that I'd found my Mom, I started wondering about my father.

I had to find him. But how?

My Mom was the link. I wasn't a miracle baby, like Jesus or Moses. Nothing like that.

I couldn't find any records of my father through the state, or any of my websites. So I had to figure out how to ask my Mom who my father was.

But Mom was tight-lipped. Every time I brought it up, a stretch of silence followed. How could I make this happen?

I'd heard she had a case of dementia, or forgetfulness, or else she just wants to disremember stuff, so I had to figure to how I was going to get that information from her. I knew that my father had passed away. So I knew she would have to be the one to tell me his name.

I might've had other ways of finding it out. I could've been sneaky, and gone behind my Mom's back. I just wanted to hear it directly from her. I didn't know exactly who he was, but I had narrowed it down to three people. So I just wanted to know who he was, and to close that chapter with the birth parents.

At the same time, I didn't want to hurt my Mom. I realized the loss of me, her son, all those years ago, must have been devastating. I had the desire to comfort her, now that I'd found her, to let her know I forgave her. I just needed to know the name of the man who fathered me.

So after the funeral blowed over a little bit, I called my Mom and said, "Do you know who my father is?"

She said, "No, I don't remember."

I said, "Hmmm." I didn't want her to think I was angry at her. So I just said, "Okay," 'cuz I didn't want to push her.

So I needed a way to flip the script.

What I did was I enlisted my sister. My sister Anna asked her, one time, who my father was, and she said she really didn't know. I didn't know if that was just her memory playing tricks with her or if she just didn't want to tell me the truth. I didn't know for sure if she was lying, I didn't know if she just didn't want to remember. Kind of hard to tell with her. She'd be good playing poker, because she never shows her hand. I knew that her sister knew, or at least I found that out later.

I don't want to say that she was lying. I wanna say that a whole lot of this was just blurry.

Next thing I did was I went on Ancestry again. I hadn't been on there for awhile, and I saw this last name Carter. And I'm like, *Okay*. There's a Carter who's a first cousin. The closest cousin I ever had was a fourth cousin, or a fifth cousin, so now I know I'm getting close.

So I took that name, and I went back to that White Pages, and started looking for Carters.

I called up my brother, and asked did he know any Carters?

He said, "The only Carter I remember is a guy who owned a photo shop in Asbury, way back in the day."

I called my sister then, and she said the same thing. She said, "Listen, there's a website called AsburyPark, something like that, on Facebook, you should go check it out."

So I went to the website. And I saw the administrator's name was Madonna Carter. So I thought, *Hmmm.*

So what I did was, I went back to White Pages, found the name Ernest Carter, and I started calling the guy. You know when you go on there, it has a list of family members and stuff, the names in the household and things like that? I tried to call Ernest Carter, but I didn't get any answer. But I saw the name Joseph Carter on the list, so I called him up.

He actually answered the phone, and I explained my story to him. He said, "I'm getting your vibe, all this ancestry and DNA stuff, and your story sounds good, and I wish you the best, but I'm gonna get my sister"—and he never did mention her name—"I'm gonna get her to see if she can help you out."

Okay, so I hung the phone up.

Two days later, I go on 23andme. I hadn't been on 23andme in a long time! And *bing!* Madonna Carter came up! So I found her number, I gave her a call, and she said, "Yes, I've been waiting for you to call me."

I said *yes!*

Now Madonna's the kind of person, her father actually gave her the photograph of all of his belongings to her, so she has all the history and pictures of Asbury. She has the history of everybody's weddings and deaths and stuff, she's like a local historian. So it was like I'd hit the jackpot!

So I told her my story, and she said *wow!* She said, "Well, me and you probably are first cousins versus siblings, because my father was an only child. So that means me and you share a grandfather and grandmother. And my grandfather's last name is Niblack."

And I said, "Okay."

And she said, "And he had, from his second marriage, eleven kids, and seven boys. I have pictures of these boys, and maybe you'll find something there."

So what I did was, I took the names of all these Niblacks—David and Oscar and George—I went with that information, and I Facetimed my sister, and I asked some questions.

"Yeah, we know some Niblacks," she said. "We heard of that name before. That name is kind of popular around here."

So I talked to my mother next. She said "Yes, I know the Niblacks."

I said, "Do you know an Oscar Niblack?"

"No," she said.

"Do you know a David Niblack?"

"Um, that sounds familiar," she said.

"How about a George Niblack?"

"No," she said, "but that sounds familiar."

I was baffled then. I groped for words. My Mom knew I was challenging her. There's a part of me that wanted to get mad but there's another part of me that regretted all the pain my birth and her abandonment of me had already put her through.

So I said, "Okay. All right, Mom."

But inside?

Inside, my mind was working on another plan.

CHAPTER 21:

OWNING IT

A couple of days went by. I said to myself, *She knows something*. Whether she wanted to admit it or not, my Mom definitely felt some fear about revealing the name of my father. Maybe, I thought, revealing it would cause her some deep and terrible hurt.

Instead of being discouraged, I went to work even harder on getting that name. I knew one thing: *This is really close*. I'm on the path but I can't prove it yet. Painful as it might be, my Mom needs to own the truth.

So what I did was, I called my Mom up again.

I said, "Listen Mom, it's very important that I know this one thing. If you want me to come down there and hold your hand, I will, and all you have to do is just tell me one time who my father is."

She said, "Okay. We'll do that."

No ducking it. No protest. No objection.

It's an hour and half to my Mom's house. So I drove up there. My sister was just leaving to go to work. She knew I was gonna broach the subject so she waved at me and said, "I'm gonna leave you two alone."

"Do you think that's safe?" I joked. And she sorta laughed at that.

So my sister left. I went in the house, and found my Mom. And I said, "Are you ready for this, Mom?"

She said, "Sure."

This was the moment I'd been dreaming of and dreading my whole life. I knew that if I pushed my Mom too hard on this, it could be one of the worst mistakes of my life.

I grabbed her hands, and we went in the kitchen. We were sitting at the kitchen table, holding each other's hands, and I said, "Mom, I know the history behind you giving me up for adoption. Now I didn't have any ill feelings, it takes a strong woman to give her child up for adoption, for a better life, because I knew you were taking care of two other kids." And I could see her tear up at that. She nodded to herself, as if she was picturing the day she gave me up, and how it had turned into something good.

I said, "I want to thank you, Mom. Thank you, because you could have voided me, but you let me live. And I wound up getting in a good home, and basically what you see today is a product of the Barnetts. I've had a good life. I've never been in jail, I joined the military, I did big things in the military, I got four kids, I got grandkids, you're a great-grandma now, all these great things are going on for me, and you're completing all this."

And so as I was holding her hand she was going down Memory Lane a little bit. She'd rub my fingers. Take my hand, rub the top of my hands. Rub each finger, like I was a little baby.

"But there's something I have to ask you," I said, "because I need to know. And I'm just gonna ask you one time."

I could feel her trembling hand in mind.

I said, "Will you give me your answer?"

And she said, "Yes."

I said, "Who is my father?

And right then I felt the shaking and the trembling stop. Very quietly I slipped my hand into hers, and held it tight. Her eyes drifted right into mine.

And she said the name. Two words.

She said, "George Niblack."

CHAPTER 22:

NOTHING WAS
THE SAME

I had a moment of fear right then. For a tense moment my Mom looked shocked, like she couldn't believe what she had just said. Like from the second she opened her mouth, and out tumbled the name *George Niblack*, nothing in our lives would ever be the same.

Turned out everything was cool. Although the way my Mom said that name just about rocked me off my chair.

After she told me the name of my father, I could see she had a little tear in her eye, so I said, "Listen. This is a happy moment. Now we've come full circle. I don't ever have to ask you this again. You have nothing to be ashamed of. I'm proud of you. I love you, and from now on we have a new start."

So I gave her a hug. She gave me a hug. And it was good.

We talked some more about life, and then my sister

wound up coming back home for some reason, and she saw us holding hands, and she said, "Aww, is everything okay, everything straight?"

I said, "Yep."

Turns out my Mom was happy she got it off her chest. I was happy she got it off her chest. I was happy to know the truth finally, after all these years of searching and not knowing.

Crazy thing happened then: I got a text message about 15 minutes after my sister came back. My other sister told me that the DNA test came back, and it showed that we were brother and sister. We were siblings. All that happened in the same day.

CHAPTER 23:

TRACING MY BLOODLINE

In the meantime, I had talked to my brother and my aunt, they told me that they remembered the name George Niblack.

"George Niblack," my aunt said, "I remember George Niblack. He was around all the time."

I said, "Okay!"

In the meantime, I had talked to Madonna, my first cousin, and I said the name George Niblack.

She said, "George?" Her mouth gaped open, astonished. "George was a really nice guy, and if he'd found out that he'd had you, he probably would have wanted to get you back."

She said George also had a daughter—actually, he had two daughters, but I guess he had one daughter, a step-daughter, he gave his name to, but he also had a daughter from his first marriage. Her name was Gwen.

I said, "Oh really? Okay."

So Madonna gave me Gwen's number. I called Gwen up, and told her the story, she said "Wow!" She agreed to take a DNA test.

So a couple of weeks went by.

During that time, I got a picture of George Niblack, from my cousin, which showed me who he was. He served in the military. He was a police officer. A corrections officer. So he was a good man. That made me happy. I don't think my mother and him had any kind of real relationship. I think it might have been just a one night stand, two night stand, I'm not sure. I told my mother I would never ask her, or talk about it.

Now.

On my father's side, the only person I knew was Madonna, my first cousin.

I got in touch with my older sister, who was a product of the first marriage. We don't like to say it, but she's a step-sister. My father gave her his name, of Niblack. And so I found out that Madonna's mother was still alive, she was turning 100 years old on the 6th of January, and they were having a little party for her on bingo night, because she does bingo. She said that's a good time for you to come.

"In the meantime," she said, "I'm going to tell my mother about you, so she can mentally prepare for you."

So January 6th came. I showed up, I was able to meet a lot of cousins. I met Ernest. Ernest was the drummer for Bruce Springsteen and the E Street Band. He lives in Asbury. He told me about my father. I talked to Joseph on the phone, I met Debbie, I met a lot of folks on the Niblack side of the family.

The thing about the Niblack family I started finding out is that it's multi-cultural. There's mulatto, there's black, there's white. So I went and found a book, it's a history, called *The Niblacks*, and I was able to trace my bloodline all the way back to like the 1700s, which is pretty cool.

About that time, my adopted father reminded me of a weird thing that happened back in the day. Something he'd just remembered.

Seems that one day years ago, my adopted father was driving up to the house. And he saw this man coming to the house. Now remember, my grandmother used to be a pastor. And she started a church. And she used to call people in, street people, and call witness to people, all kinds of people, and talk to them about Christ.

So my father, he knew my grandmother used to do stuff like that. So he used to make sure that people who went in the house were on the up and up, to make sure she was safe.

So this tall man, about 6 foot 4 according to my father, he's coming up onto the porch. And my father's pulling into the driveway at the same time.

So he goes onto the porch right behind the man. Just wanted to make sure that this individual was good to go. Said he remembered the guy had black hair, curly black hair.

Anyway my father checked the guy out, and decided the guy was cool. So my father went upstairs. My grandmother came in, proceeded to talk to this individual, said, "What can I do for you, how can I help you?"

And this man looked around the room. The way my

grandmother had the room set up was with family pictures on the piano and stuff. And the man looked around, and was scanning the area, and then he said:

"How is Kevin doing?"

Like that.

My grandmother narrowed her eyes. She studied the man with his black, curly hair.

And she said, "Kevin is doing fine, he's in high school. How do you know Kevin?"

And the man looked around, like he was weighing everything he saw, and said, "I'm glad that he's doing fine."

And he walked out the door. He left. Just like that.

Now. Fast forward.

When I found who my father was, I told my adopted father. I said, "Pops, I remember that story you told me. I'm gonna send you some pictures." And he looked at the picture, and he said, "That was the guy that came into the house that day!"

So I'm like, "Really?"

So somehow or other George Niblack found out I had been born, in later years. So he came down to visit, because I was his biological son, and because he used to be a police officer he had ways of finding out stuff about folks. So he found the house, and wanted to drop by and see if everything was cool, and that I was doing really, really good. And he met my father.

The weird thing is, George Niblack and all his siblings are 6 foot 4 and above. The tallest one being 7 feet. Apparently I got my height from my mother, since I'm only 5 foot 8! But I got all the good hair, like my father.

But my father remembered him. Because he had that jet-black hair. And my father said, "I'm glad he didn't try to take you away that day, 'cuz we woulda been fighting!"

CHAPTER 24:

MY CHASE COMES FULL CYCLE

Fast forward a few months…

I'm still meeting more relatives. I'm meeting people on Facebook, I'm meeting cousins. Seems Niblack is a very unusual name so usually anybody with that last name is a relative.

I did a DNA test on my Mom. So now we're finding out more things about her side of the family. Like I said, I already knew I was from St. Kitts, the whole West Indies. Actually from the Bahamas all the way to Trinidad is basically where my bloodline from both sides of my family come from. So it's like that completeness.

I found another cousin, another first cousin, one of my father's siblings' daughters, named Anita. The weird thing is, I found her, and she had no connection with anybody. So now I brought *her* into the family. I got her to start talking to folks, meeting family, stuff like that. She's in Asbury too.

Weird, right? Now *I'm* the one connecting people to my family!

It's been an ongoing thing with meeting different people in all these different places. I got folks living on the East Coast, and out West, in Washington State, and in Portland, Oregon. Hopefully I'll be able to hop on a plane and meet them one day when I go visit my grandkids.

You know, that's the point I'm at right now. Just still meeting people. Experiencing new things.

One of the other things that I did, the day I met my parents and all that stuff, I set up a thing with my adopted parents, the Barnetts, in the Poconos of Pennsylvania. And I talked to my adopted dad, and told him what I did, and he was all happy. I talked to my brothers, you know, from the family that raised me, and I said I want you to come and meet my birth family.

So I made a date. October 22, 2016. And I got a truck, and I picked my bloodline up, and I took 'em up to the Poconos. We had a big celebration of everybody coming together. And everybody got along! Everybody was happy! I was able to sit together with my mom who raised me, and my mom who birthed me. It was *amazing!* Siblings I grew up with were there with siblings I didn't even know. Everybody was calling each other brothers and sisters.

That was a nice day.

And believe it or not, my sister on my mother's side, and my sister on my father's side, found out they'd gone to high school and grammar school together, and they're graduated together! It's true—they knew each other, prior to me. Cool, right?

All because I said to my sister on my father's side, "Listen, I have another sister named Gwen. Gwen Niblack."

"Get outta here!" my sister Anna said. Her eyes got wide, as if she didn't believe what I'd just told her. "I went to school with a girl named Gwen Niblack!"

Next thing I knew they started texting back and forth. Come to find out they actually went to school together back in the day, and they were actually friends!

Lot of weird things like that've been happening. Lots of hits and misses. Lot of people saying, "Yeah, I knew that person...yeah I know that brother...I heard of that sister..."

So that felt like it was the completion, the full cycle, of the chase.

If this part of the story sounds too good to be true, brace yourselves. Because it gets even better. Because this is where the twists and turns in the story took a dark turn, and strengthened my belief that anything is possible. And the dream of my life turned into a wild adventure.

CHAPTER 25:

LOSING MOM

On the 8th of June, I received a phone call from my sister Anna, begging me to meet her at Monmouth Medical Center in New Jersey. Seems my Mom had been admitted with what they thought was high blood pressure, and suffered what looked like a heart attack.

After I hung up the phone, I was in a daze. *Heart attack?* Nothing can prepare you for the shock of hearing your Mom might be gone. The news hit me like a punch in the gut. It jolted me as I thought of her dying before I even got to know her.

Losing Mom wouldn't just break my heart. It would put a big hole in in the world. It would reopen the hole I'd worked so hard to fill.

Immediately I sent some emails out to work, saying I wouldn't be in, and that I was heading up to Asbury to be with my Mom.

Monmouth Medical Center's in Long Branch. About two

hours away, via the New Jersey Turnpike. As I drove a small voice in my head whispered that this visit to see my Mom might be our last. I'd just met her, and now she might be gone forever. She'd had a good run of 88 years. Maybe this was the end.

I was upset. I didn't want to lose her, because I'd just found her. Ironically she was supposed to come up to visit me that weekend. So I was scared, I know she's 88, she's on borrowed time, and the next month was my birthday—yep, my birthday was just around the corner. So I was just praying for another year. I just wanted to hear the words "Happy birthday!" come out of my Mom's mouth. That was going to be like the perfect gift, for me.

I didn't know what to expect, when I got to the hospital. But I was kind of relieved when I saw my family there. I embraced my relatives in my Mom's hospital room. My Mom was lying there, in bed—she was happy to see me, she told everybody I was coming, and all that good stuff.

To my surprise, I found my Mom cheerful and free from pain. Maybe because of the medications she'd been given.

Her blood pressure was very high. My brother John said that's caused him to take her to the hospital.

He said once they got to the hospital, they had problems taking her blood. "The reason they kept her," John explained, "is because they thought she might have had a heart attack." What it actually was, according to the doctors, is just extremely high blood pressure. And so they were trying to make sure that it stayed at a certain level, before releasing her. But at the same time, she was very nervous and confused by a lot of things. And that prompted them into thinking she was having a stroke.

But she wasn't having a stroke. It's just her slight case of dementia. So a lot of questions they were trying to ask her, she couldn't answer.

That's why I ended up staying down there. I stayed around Asbury for a couple of days, to make sure my Mom was okay and good to go. Just see where I could help as much as possible.

Day after day I sat with her, reflecting on all those years I'd missed her, and how I'd finally found her. I realized how my life had come full circle. Here my mother was, lying in a hospital bed, just like she probably was the day I'd been born. Only here I am, a grown man now, sitting at her bedside, feeding her, nursing her, cradling her, patting her on the cheek. And praying for her.

Couple of days later, she went home. Overall she's feeling pretty good now. She fell down, one day. She didn't drink water, like she was supposed to, because of the medication. Luckily she didn't hit her head.

The good thing about it is that she was able to take all these tests. So we know there's nothing physically wrong with her now. She didn't have any history of heart problems. Just high blood pressure.

It was a little scary, after all I'd gone through to find my Mom. But she made it through. So it's all good.

It was a good weekend. The fact that I was able to spend time with my blood family, three days in a row, and at the same time seeing my Mom, it wound up being a good weekend.

All the bad things in the past were behind us now, and the potential for an awesome future was out in front of us.

CHAPTER 26:

MOTHER'S DAY

Sunday, May 14, 2017 was Mother's Day. The day of the year when mothers are honored by their children.

Excited about this whole brand-new experience of finding my Mom, I was able to do something I'd never done in my life—buy my birth mom a Mother's Day card! Who knew this day would ever come to pass?

57 years ago, I was left on a porch for dead. Now, 57 years later, I'm going up and down the aisles in a card shop, and like so many millions of Americans I'm hunting for the perfect Mother's Day card to give to my Mom.

I can't help but laugh, thinking about it.

It's been a crazy year.

I was able to sing happy birthday to my mother, for the first time in my life. We had a little dinner, up in Asbury Park, that was very moving for me. Then I was able to go pick out that Mother's Day card. And I mailed her some flowers. But the family celebrations just kept on rollin'. My sister got married, and she gave me and my other brother the honor of being witnesses, and signing her wedding certificate.

At this stage in my life, I'd done just about everything. I served 20 years in the U.S. military. I'd fought for my country in battle. I went to college and earned an AA, a BS and an MS. I ran a full marathon, and finished in the top half. I received a 2nd-degree black belt in Hapkido, and earned sixteen medals and thirteen top decorations from the Army. I'd experienced the pleasure of seeing my children born, and started my own foundation, LivingMyShadows, to help other folks overcome their obstacles. But I had never experienced the sound of my own voice crying out "Happy birthday!" and "Happy Mother's Day, Mom!" to my birth mom.

And after that, according to my sister Anna, my mother's spirits have been up, she's been uplifted, she ain't grouchy or grumbling no more. Seems she is really happy to have me in her life. We've started talking nearly every day. Sometimes if I miss a couple of days she says, "What's wrong, where's Kevin, how come he ain't calling me?"

That's pretty much my definition of a happy ending to my story.

Only it's not the end.

CHAPTER 27:

MY FIRST BIRTHDAY

My 57TH birthday was July 30, 2017.

In reality, you might say it was my very *first* birthday.

When you're unwanted—when you've spent your whole life living in the shadows—you can only dream about things like this.

We held my birthday on a Saturday. It was July 29th—that's right, a day early. That's to surprise me on the day before, because everybody in my family was off on Saturday.

They set everything up at the Hampton Inn in Neptune, New Jersey.

Who was there? My adopted family, the Barnetts, were there. And my birth family on both sides, my Mom's family and my father's—they were there. My wife was there, too. Whole lot of other family members. About 25 to 30 people, waiting to surprise me.

Did they surprise me? I'll let you figure it out…

I thought we were having a little family birthday party at a restaurant. My sister Anna, she told me I'd be meeting a few new family members afterward, at the hotel.

So my brother John drove me and my wife Sharon to the hotel.

So as we got into the hotel, I had no idea something was up. My sister Anna told me that there were a few family members, waiting for me around the corner. "In that room," she said, pointing it out. And as soon as I went around the corner, that's when they jumped out and yelled, "Surprise!"

I was astonished at seeing all these people. My heart was pounding and my legs had turned to water. Everybody rushed up to shake my hand and kiss me. And my birth mother—she was sitting there, smiling and laughing at me, and so I gave her a big hug.

More and more relatives approached me, one cousin and then another, patting me on the back. *Where did they all come from?* I wondered. And then I saw—

They had a birthday cake with my name on it.

They had bottles of water with my name and stuff on it.

I stared and stared around the room, just taking everything in. I didn't notice something else until I 'd been there for about 2 minutes. But I started listening, and I realized they were playing this song that I have on my web page. It's a song that I also use for my opening when I do motivational speaking. It's a song by Drake, "Started From The Bottom"—

Started from the bottom now we're here

Started from the bottom now the whole team here—

They had that song playing. And as soon as I noticed, and

those lyrics started tumbling through my head, I thought to myself, *Man, that's pretty cool.*

My sister Gwen was there. My adopted sister who I grew up with was there too, so I had like all three sisters together. And my brother, and my aunts, and some cousins, and some friends who were there from out of town.

They sang happy birthday to me. They had a whole bunch of food there. I gave everybody a glimpse of what this book would look like. Told them a really short version of my first ten years of life, and that basically this was my first birthday, that I'd been looking forward to and dreaming about for 57 years. And I was finally able to sing happy birthday with my birth mother and my family, for the very first time in my life.

My Mom sang happy birthday to me, holding my hands. It was touching! People were crying. I shed a couple of tears, you know.

Then I had some birthday presents, and a bunch of cards, and a lot of money. I don't understand why they gave me money! Yeah, so it was cool, it was pretty good.

I found out later that my wife and my brother, they knew the whole time what was coming. I'm the only one that didn't know. And it turned out great. People were happy. Family members who I'd pulled out of the corners and the wood-work—who were disconnected from family—I was able to get them together. They came. They enjoyed themselves. Hilarious laughter rocked the room. So it was really wonderful.

And the caveat off of that? Me and my wife came up with the idea to have a cookout. A barbecue cookout in late August. About 50 people were supposed to come—my birth mom, my wife's side of the family, the adopted family I grew up with, and my father's family. I had people coming from Connecticut, from D.C., from New Jersey, from the Poconos. I told 'em all to bring a dish and we're gonna have some music and a good time. We'll have name tags so people can mingle, get to know family members they've never met or they don't get a chance to converse with very much. I also had two more people I found through Ancestry.com who are blood relatives. There was one I was gonna meet for the very first time, who's been trying to find his father. So his story sounds just like mine.

It was a good month of July, and a good month of August. A good summer, and a good year. For the most part, that is.

I had some deaths in the family. My mother-in-law passed away. And my cousin and my nephew passed on, too. But that's part of life, I guess. I've been looking forward to seeing my grandkids in Washington State in August.

So that's it for the birthday party. People were talking about it for weeks. They're still talking about it! I've seen pictures on Facebook, pictures on Instagram.

Oh, one other thing:

My Mom bought me a birthday card. I also got some New York Giants gear from my sister. I got money from my mother and sister. I got gift cards.

But the card from my Mom is what blew my mind. I opened it up, and held it in my hands, and read the words over and over:

> You're such a stand-up guy. With a quick smile, and a
> good heart. While it'd be nice to take credit for all of your

great qualities, the truth is that's just who you are, and how you've always been.

Then inside, it said:

You're simply wonderful, a wonderful son, and the years only make you more so.
Happy birthday.
Love, Mom.

That's it!

It felt unbelievable to have my Mom sing happy birthday to me, after all these years. She was standing right in front of me. Singing "Happy birthday" with everybody. It felt like I was dreaming—except that when I woke up, my dream came true! Like I was dreaming for 57 years. I gave Mom the first piece of my birthday cake, too! She was happy. You know, it just felt terrific.

It was a birthday wish that came true, so now I gotta think of another wish!

CHAPTER 28:

SHADOWS DISAPPEARING AT THE LIGHT OF DAY

So how do I feel today, at the end of this long journey to find my bloodline, my birth mom and dad, my family?

What are my thoughts today, as I'm writing this book?

Today I feel pretty much complete. I'm grateful that everything happened the way it happened. I wish it had happened earlier, but of course I can't guarantee that I'd have been able to handle all this, when I was younger. I think it's all the right time for this to happen. My wife has been here for me the whole time, and she's been my support and my rock. She's been strong enough to handle her own loss in life, and the losses that have happened prior to meeting my family.

I have a chance to love my Mom now. To live the life I'd never had. I couldn't ask for anything more.

I'm continuing to digest what's happened during the last

10 years. Sure, the past still hurts. I have scars from the past, but I will always have those scars, and I've turned them to my advantage and used those scars to make myself stronger. The losses I've experienced still eat at me, but that's life. We all experience loss. I try to keep that in mind.

Like my sister Anna said, they suffered loss, too. We lost my brother Kenny, and it seemed like according to her I kinda like replaced him, a little bit, in spirit and in body, because I look like him, I act like him, we have pretty much the same personality.

Maybe I wasn't lucky enough to be welcomed into my mother and father's lives from Day One. But the Barnetts made me feel like family nonetheless.

I think there's a reason why all this is happening to me. Bringing people together, bringing all the families together, bringing in-laws together, and being able to spearhead that. It's just a blessing. I feel blessed to be blessed, and to bless other people. I can't deny that sometimes it's overwhelming.

Sometimes I can't cry.

And sometimes I do cry.

Sometimes I laugh and I shake my head because I used to think I was the unluckiest guy in the world and now I'm the luckiest guy in the world.

I'm still helping people on Facebook and on Ancestry. I'm trying to help people find their loved ones, and I wanna get into that a little bit more. I'm just blessed to have the privilege to touch others with my story, and lift them up. That's the only way I can say it.

It feels like I'm on Cloud 59.

It's like I'm a brand-new me. A brand-new Kevin.

I think back on my childhood full of abuse and torture and mistreatment, and I see my life now as something I created out of my dreams.

"There is no greater agony," Maya Angelou once said, "than bearing an untold story inside of you."

My story is no longer untold.

And I hope that in knowing my story, you will feel inspired to push harder, in your own life, to be all you can be. No matter what anybody else tells you. If you've got a passion, or something or somebody that's missing in your life, don't give up the hunt. Don't let depression, defeat, fear, or rejection stop you. You are the author of your own life. You can change the plot, and rewrite your story any way you choose.

Never surrender on that dream of yours. Listen to the voice that tells you to keep going.

I'm all about claiming your dreams, even when others doubt you. I overcame the impossible. You can do the same with your dreams.

My story is out there now. My story is finished.

You've got a story too. You're the author. You're the driver and your dream is the roadmap.

Now go get it!

FAMILY PHOTOS

Sister Gwen and my birth father.

Me and my brothers and sis.

Meeting my birth mom for the first time.

Aunt Audrey and my sister Anna.

Meeting the Niblack family (my birth father's side).

My Pops and my birth mother and her sister.

My birth father's only living sibling GG (100 years old).

Brother Johnny and me.

Sister Anna and me.

Brother Johnny, birth mom, me, sister Anna,
and my wife Sharon.

Group pic at the soul food restaurant.

My wife Sharon and Step-Daughter Samantha

"My young men,
top left to right Kevin & Isaiah,
bottom left to right Charles & Darrius

Dad, me, and Mommy.

IN GRATITUDE

Special thanks to my wife Sharon F. Pelham, for putting up with all the craziness that she had to endure during the process. And thank you to the U.S. Army.

CONTACT

My life story can help you overcome obstacles and be successful in your own life. As a motivational speaker, I energize people to meet the challenges of the world around them.

Don't let obstacles stop you.

If you are interested in learning more, please visit my website:

www.livingmyshadows.org

Or contact my foundation:

LivingMyShadows, LLC
560 Peoples Plaza, #290
Newark, DE. 19702
PHONE: (302) 353-9841
EMAIL: livingmyshadows@gmail.com

CPSIA information can be obtained
at www.ICGtesting.com
Printed in the USA
JSHW042018150323
38972JS00001B/15